JFK and the Reagan Revolution

Lawrence Kudlow and Brian Domitrovic

JFK AND THE
REAGAN REVOLUTION

A Secret History of American Prosperity

To Cynthia + Ray

PORTFOLIO

Larry Kudlow

An imprint of Penguin Random House LLC
375 Hudson Street
New York, New York 10014

INSERT CREDITS

Abbie Rowe, White House Photographs, John F. Kennedy Presidential Library and Museum, Boston: page 1 (top and bottom); Robert L. Knudsen (Robert LeRoy), John F. Kennedy Presidential Library and Museum, Boston: page 2 (top), page 3 (top), page 5 (bottom); Getty Images/Bettmann: page 2 (middle), page 4 (middle), page 5 (top), page 6 (top); HUP, Stanley S. Surrey (1), Harvard University Archives: page 2 (bottom); Getty Images/Paul Schutzer: page 3 (bottom); University of Chicago Library: page 4 (top); John F. Kennedy Presidential Library: page 4 (bottom); AP Photo: page 6 (bottom); Associated Press/Scott Applewhite: page 7 (top); courtesy of the Ronald Reagan Library: page 7 (bottom); photographs courtesy of Lawrence Kudlow: page 8 (top and bottom)

ISBN 9781595231147 (hardcover)
ISBN 9780698162839 (e-book)

Printed in the United States of America
1   3   5   7   9   10   8   6   4   2

Book design by Francesca Belanger

Contents

Introduction

Fifteen-plus years into the twenty-first century, Americans are in a sour mood. They are cranky. Unhappy. Pessimistic (something Americans almost never are). They are trashing politicians of both parties. They are looking for scapegoats—immigrants, foreign trade, the top 1 percent, Wall Street traders, fat cats.

But if you take a step back twenty to thirty years, to the 1980s and 1990s, there was scarcely any incitement to class warfare. Whatever prejudices there were against foreigners ("Japan, Inc.") were fading fast, and people were more interested in working than blaming. Americans were optimistic, psyched. The mood of the country was up.

The big difference between the years of the 2000s and the two decades before? Economic growth. In the 1980s and 1990s, the economy of the United States was growing rapidly—4 percent per year for long stretches. Forty-four million new jobs appeared from 1983 to 2000, an increase of 50 percent in total employment in a good deal less than a generation's time. The stock market went up fifteenfold. The effects were felt broadly: savings and nest eggs grew enormously as the average family became a fifth again as rich in 1999 as compared with half a generation before. If these well-established trends had held, untold prosperity would have settled in as the permanent condition of the American people in the twenty-first century.

That boom, immense and extended as it was, did not, of course, last. Since the peak year, 2000, economic growth in the United States has averaged 1.9 percent per year—barely enough to cover the yearly increase in population. If you subtract the growth of government and just measure the growth of the private, or "real," economy, the number

1

is even more pathetic—1.4 percent per year. Private-sector employment has inched upward at the achingly slow rate of half a percent per year since 2000. Ten million fewer Americans are employed today than there would be if the trends of the 1980s and 1990s had been sustained; the average family makes $10,000 less comparatively. It was not even the Great Recession that dragged down all these numbers very much. Economic growth since the bottom of the bust in 2009 has been 2 percent per year, making the recovery one of the weakest ever. The prosperity that drove the optimism of the 1980s and 1990s is not even a shadow of itself in America today.

Instead of economic growth, throughout the fifteen-plus years of this new millennium we have been experiencing a historically unusual period of stagnation. Americans don't like it, it does not suit them, and they are wondering what has happened. As the memory of prosperity recedes, Americans are starting to lose one of their essential traits, optimism. As events from the Occupy Wall Street movement of several years ago to the menacing university protests of 2015 to the combative election campaigns of 2016 have shown, the national temper is drawing short, people are getting at one another's throats, the search is on for unconventional saviors, and divisiveness and conflict, and sometimes a little resignation, are all around. This is not the way America is supposed to be.

Economic growth—isn't that something that can only be experienced in short spaces, too unusual and intense a thing to be sustained permanently? Not so: economic growth can be sustained, and for the comprehensive betterment of humanity, as the American experience in particular over the centuries has proved resoundingly.

Since the very dawn of civilization, the resources available to human societies have remained fixed. We have the planet Earth, its crust and atmosphere, along with sunlight from our star. The thing that has changed over the course of history is people's ingenuity in using those fixed resources. When we have the *freedom*—as the great economist Milton Friedman always told us—to get better at learning how to work and how to use resources, something almost miraculous happens. We make things more easily, while using fewer resources as inputs, and we make better and more useful things—often things we had not realized we were capable of producing in the first place.

This is what economic growth is: abundance coincident with fulfillment and happiness, all of us becoming flush with the good fruits of our ingenuity, more prosperous, more satisfied in our work and in our leisure, in our lives here on earth. Clearly economic growth is not worthy only because of its material benefits. It is a sign that humanity is functioning at its highest level. Growth means that we are being good stewards of, and are applying the limitless abilities of the human mind to, the earth's resources. It means that we are equipping ourselves to be good neighbors, since as the economic pie gets bigger, so can everyone's piece of it. Growth here in America means that our great country continues to be an exemplar to the rest of the world, drawing the talented and ambitious to these shores and inspiring emulation in untold places. Growth means that the United States is strong and secure—not only because growth confers power, but because it prompts others to admire and join us. Economic growth is human, it is impressive, it is fulfilling, and it is good.

The American people have always (until this strange new millennium) proved themselves adept at economic growth. In the nineteenth century, the country boomed as it attracted immigrants by the millions, overturned slavery, and experienced an increase in the standard of living unimaginable to previous generations. About 125 years ago, in the thick of the Industrial Revolution, the United States became the world's largest economy. It has never lost that status, even through today's stagnation.

In the twentieth century, the success powered on. Innumerable Americans lived lives, as the essayist Tom Wolfe once put it (referring to the lavish monarch of old-regime France), that "would have made the Sun King blink." The meaningful work, the spacious homes, the cars, the vacations, the opportunities that the *average* inhabitant of this country had as a matter of course throughout much of the twentieth century were unparalleled. There was so much widespread income and leisure in the "American Century," as it came to be known, that to make a comparison to the *richest* people of ages past was unfair.[1]

This is quite a legacy of prosperity, and we are now, in the sluggish 2000s, in danger of forsaking it. Even worse, forsaking our legacy of prosperity means forsaking our legacy of life, liberty, and the pursuit of happiness—and of serving as a beacon of freedom and opportunity globally. The idea that America can be America without economic growth is preposterous. Our place in the world, our care for the poor, our innovation all will degrade if we continue in the economic mediocrity we have been living with of late.

The reason for stagnation is that our nation has forgotten two key truths. The first truth is that the engine of economic growth is the private sector. As people seek to provide for themselves and improve the world around them, by pursuing projects as entrepreneurs, or by joining such projects through employment at a business, they become ever better at working with the fixed resources of the earth. Something special happens in turn. What the great free-market economist F. A. Hayek called "spontaneous order"—that of economic bounty and interpersonal cooperation—comes about.

The second truth is that the government's most important responsibility is to make sure that growth happens, and this is done by getting out of the way. The government does not need to stimulate demand; businesses and entrepreneurs know how to do that through innovation. Providing a safety net for those who are not able to enjoy the growth is a small matter in a booming economy, and in any case economic growth fosters a spirit of cooperation in American citizens. Even providing for national defense is less important than ensuring growth, since economic growth inspires the world to emulate America instead of fighting with it.

These two truths have kept America prosperous, and yet here we are in this mediocre new millennium. For pushing nearly twenty years now, government has not gotten out of the way. Rather, it has forgotten—or chosen not to grasp—its main responsibility. It has stuck its snout into the real economy to an uncommon degree.

The list of ways the government has interfered is long, substantial, and depressing. The Sarbanes-Oxley Act of 2002 imposed deadening regulations on businesses, particularly small ones. The Dodd-Frank Act of 2010 did the same thing to banks, again hurting small ones most. The Environmental Protection Agency, the Internal Revenue Service, Department of Labor compliance agencies, and Obamacare are smothering the private sector. Government spending at all levels has zoomed up by 45 percent in real terms since the turn of the millennium, an increase twice as large as that of the private sector. Effective tax rates are higher than they were in 2000. As for the Federal Reserve, it has never been more activist than in the 2000s. The economy has responded to all of this in clear fashion: by not growing.

While some may suggest that government interference has brought other benefits, we cannot lose sight of a reality that the great supply-side economist Arthur B. Laffer has long emphasized: people respond to incentives. Tax and regulate something more, you get less of it. Make the real value of a profit stream questionable by destabilizing the dollar, and you get less capital devoted to maintaining that profit stream. When government gets calm and limited, people respond by taking risks, and working and investing for the clear prospect of rewards.

Economic growth is the single most important result of and justification for America's free-market capitalist system. In these strange, sluggish, unperforming, and uncharacteristic years of the 2000s, Americans have begun to forget that growth is central to what we are about. To reclaim it, government must let the private sector return to being its natural and productive self.

Fortunately, we have a model to follow as we seek to return to being a nation of growth. It is the John F. Kennedy–Ronald Reagan model. It is the model of getting the government restrained and modest in its two key areas of economic policy: fiscal policy and monetary policy. Both Kennedy and Reagan identified *substantially cutting income tax rates and getting the dollar strong and stable* as the specific policy mix that would let the private sector, which is to say the real economy, thrive.

Most of us are well aware that Ronald Reagan was a tax cutter and that the horrible "stagflation"—weak economic growth in the context of prodigious price inflation—of the 1970s and early 1980s came to an end in the first years of his presidency. We are even aware, and correctly, that Bill Clinton used that model to foster prosperity in the decade after Reagan, when the Republican Congress guided him toward the policy mix. What is generally unknown, however, and what is the subject of this book, is that President John F. Kennedy in the early 1960s not only used but largely pioneered the same model. Kennedy came into office during a period in which growth was only a little better than today's. His presidency launched the United States on one of the longest and greatest economic expansions in its history, one that lasted until his successors forsook his model, and then repeated itself two decades hence thanks to the emulation of JFK by Reagan.

It was a policy mix of tax rate cuts and a strong and stable dollar, the essence of governmental restraint and modesty in fiscal and monetary matters. Over the decades of the past half century and more, when this approach, adopted to perfection by JFK, has been maintained, the country has seen historic prosperity. When the approach has been forsaken, a stagnation that does not befit the prosperous traditions of this country has ensued. If Kennedy thought it urgent to "get this country moving again"—his most prominent campaign slogan as he ran for president—in the slow-growth conditions of 1960, how much more relevant is his message today.

If Americans had known this history, we probably would have tried the JFK-Reagan policy mix again years ago in our slow-growth 2000s. We would have kept tax rates low. We would have maintained a strong and stable dollar. And as a result, we would have traded stagnation for expansion, just as we did in the twentieth century, whenever enlightened leadership confronted the lack of economic growth.

And yet this history has been obscured. Today's liberals and progressives act as if tax rate cuts and a meaningful dollar are shockingly far-right policies that were not put into practice in the 1960s, failed when tried in the 1980s, and could work only in a dreamworld. Democrats who are proud to claim Kennedy are horrified by those who would implement his policies today. A concerted effort has been made to present Kennedy as a Keynesian, when the opposite is in fact true.

To be sure, Kennedy did not come to his tax-rate-cut, strong-and-stable-dollar economic policy immediately. He had to weigh the claims of his advisers, some of whom were Keynesian professors, some of whom, such as Treasury Secretary (and a Republican) C. Douglas Dillon, held firm that tax rate cuts and a good dollar were essential to economic progress. The maturation of Kennedy's economic views took time, and Kennedy committed to pursuing a major tax rate cut in particular only after he experimented with Keynesian spending and got burned by a major drop in the stock market and forecasts of an imminent recession. But commit he did. Neither his policies nor their results, including how they inspired the supply-side economics of the Reagan administration, can be erased. The story of the germination, implementation, results, influence, and at times misrepresentation of the JFK economic policy, above all his signature tax rate cut, is what unfolds in the pages that follow.

We two authors came to write this book because of our concern for

this country's economy and for Kennedy's hidden history. Larry Kudlow grew up, like many of the 1960s generation, smitten with JFK.
When he worked under Paul Volcker at the New York Federal Reserve
in the 1970s, and then in the Reagan administration as associate economics director at the Office of Management and Budget in the 1980s,
it was clear to him that redoing what Kennedy had achieved would be
the best option the federal government could pursue in the face of
stagflation and the fading of the American dream. And that is what
Reagan and Volcker did.

And yet for years, on television, on the radio, in the mail, at dinners and events, and on social media, Larry has had to endure claims
that the JFK tax cut and policy mix were completely different from
what Reagan had tried. Larry is one of many Reaganites who have
received the equivalent of cease-and-desist orders from self-appointed
representatives of the Kennedy clan, who say that JFK would be ap-
palled to hear his name supporting the tax cut proposals of Reagan, or
George W. Bush, or former Massachusetts senator Scott Brown. Yet as
Brown showed in his successful 2010 campaign to fill the seat of JFK's
departed brother Ted Kennedy, all you have to do is play the video-
tape of JFK speaking on tax rate cuts in the 1960s to face accusations of
unfairness. Real evidence, that of history, drawn from archives and all
sorts of public sources, makes it clear that latter-day tax rate cutters
who have called on JFK's example have done so with justification.

The second of us authors, Brian Domitrovic, is a professional historian. Several years ago, he wrote what has become the standard history of supply-side economics, of the Reagan revolution in economic
policy, a book called *Econoclasts* (2009). Something that Brian touched
on in that book was how the earliest exponents of the tax-rate-cut/
sound-dollar policy mix in the 1970s—the people who came to influence Reagan in this direction—played roles in the rise of the JFK policy mix too, in the 1960s.

Both of us, Larry and Brian, are full-throated advocates of economic growth, free-market capitalism—"the best path to prosperity," as Larry says—and the American dream. "King dollar and tax cuts" has been another of Larry's taglines on television and the radio and is far from being just some slogan. The combination of a strong and stable dollar with big, permanent, across-the-board tax rate cuts is specifically the policy mix that has generated the whopping share of American economic growth since the inception of the Federal Reserve and the income tax in the fateful year of 1913.

This model, which JFK made his own and installed as precedent in the early 1960s, is the secret not merely to restoring economic growth but by virtue of that attainment to eliminating the problems we might think insoluble. Budget deficits, the retirement crisis, student loans, unaffordable health care, poor schools, inner cities—all these things will fade away as lasting economic growth takes hold. The fruits of economic growth, especially of the American variety, are so abundant that the difficulties born of privation and scarcity cannot persist.

John F. Kennedy's example reminds us that this is so. Like Reagan, Kennedy wanted Americans not to lean on government to limp through life but to go out in the economy and take a rip at the ball. If the government did not get in the way, Kennedy and Reagan believed that a wholesome general prosperity would come about, wiping away division and cynicism and engendering a national happiness. We badly need reminding of this ideal in these pitifully slow-growth years, a now nearly two-decade era of economic mediocrity that does not befit this country and its traditions. So it is to the odyssey that JFK undertook to return America to economic growth, and the example and inspiration it gave to an optimistic clutch of reformers including Ronald Reagan in the generation hence, that we now turn.

Chapter 1

STORMY WEATHER

The air hung heavy on Thursday, January 19, 1961, as America's youngest-ever president-elect spent his final day preparing to take office. As John F. Kennedy spent the morning meeting with the outgoing president, Dwight D. Eisenhower, a storm was gathering. By nightfall, a thunderous blizzard would set in, interfering with inauguration eve festivities and leaving ten thousand cars abandoned on the streets of metropolitan Washington, D.C. But for now, a different storm occupied the youthful statesman: an economic one.

This was the second time Eisenhower and Kennedy had gotten together since Kennedy's narrow election victory over Eisenhower's vice president, Richard M. Nixon, the previous November. It was Eisenhower's last chance to brief his successor, and he touched on several of the worrisome matters facing the nation. He advised Kennedy to put troops in Laos to stifle the Ho Chi Minh Trail, which North Vietnam was developing to make a push into South Vietnam. JFK would not take this advice.

Kennedy did take Eisenhower's economic concerns seriously. Ike insisted that Kennedy do something about the increasing degree to which foreigners were coming to the U.S. Treasury to trade in their dollars for gold at the guaranteed rate of $35 per ounce. The $1.5 billion in yearly "dollar dumps" by foreigners appeared to indicate a growing lack of global confidence in American economic leadership and performance. If left unchecked, the flight from the dollar could precipitate an economic crisis at home and endanger foreign policy goals. JFK summoned his treasury secretary–designate, C. Douglas Dillon, to this portion of the meeting. Dillon's presence surely conveyed the message that JFK was taking Ike seriously on the issue. Dillon was a Republican and until two weeks before had been Eisenhower's undersecretary of state.

When Kennedy left the White House just before noon, he headed
to the residence of a friend for a briefing by his incoming labor secretary, Arthur Goldberg. Goldberg told him that the number of Americans who were unemployed was rising sharply, possibly to the level of
5.5 million, a staggering 50 percent jump in the space of one year. Kennedy left the home where he had met Goldberg and assured the press,
"We'll have something to say in a few days" about how to tackle the
unemployment problem. Then he was off to a lunch at a gathering of
the leaders of the labor unions making up the AFL-CIO. After a standing ovation on his entrance, Kennedy told this group that the major
challenge he faced was "maintaining our standing in the free world."
George Meany, the AFL-CIO president, relayed afterward that Kennedy had insisted that "the Nation's standing . . . depended on the domestic economy, and that his first concern was," quoting the
president-elect, "to 'try to get this country moving forward again.'"[1]

Kennedy was talking about the sluggish economy, but the next day
hundreds of military men who had been brought in for the inauguration
took that charge literally as they shoveled out the nearly two hundred
cars that had been abandoned in the snow on Pennsylvania Avenue.
They succeeded in clearing the way for the inauguration, and right on
schedule, on a platform in front of the Capitol, Kennedy delivered his
enormously and justly famous inaugural address in the clear cold.

The fame of Kennedy's greatest line—"ask not what your country
can do for you—ask what you can do for your country"—has overshad-
owed the fact that the first issue, foreign or domestic, that John F. Kennedy brought up in his inaugural address was poverty. "For man holds
in his mortal hands the power to abolish all forms of human poverty,"
he said, reading the second sentence of the second paragraph of the
1,366-word script, after he had dispensed with the salutations.

Kennedy returned to the theme three further times in the fourteen-
minute address. At the four-minute mark, he said, "If a free society
cannot help the many who are poor, it cannot save the few who are

rich." A moment later, speaking of our "sister republics south of our border," he called for "a new alliance for progress—to assist free men and free governments in casting off the chains of poverty." And five minutes after that, he called on the nation "to bear the burden of a long twilight struggle . . . a struggle against the common enemies of man: tyranny, poverty, disease, and war itself."

As Kennedy had composed the speech with the help of his aide Theodore Sorensen in the weeks prior to the inauguration, he had told Sorensen to identify and apply the "secret" of Abraham Lincoln's Gettysburg Address. One of those secrets was addressing the most pressing concerns of the moment, and it was no accident that Kennedy devoted, comparatively, so many precious words to poverty in an inaugural address that he was determined to make a historic one. At the time of his inauguration, nearly five and a half million Americans were out of work, eligible for an average of $31 a week, for half a year, in unemployment insurance.[2]

The recession responsible for the growing unemployment of January 1961 had hit the previous April, the month before Kennedy stunned the political establishment by winning the Democratic primary in West Virginia, and the recession itself was only half of the problem with the American economy. The other half was that it was neither unprecedented nor surprising. Recessions were becoming rather the norm over this part of an era that we often today refer to as "postwar prosperity." The 1960–61 recession came on the heels of two that had already occurred during the eight years of the Eisenhower administration. At the time of Kennedy's inauguration in January 1961, the United States had spent twenty-seven of the previous ninety months in economic contraction.

Yes, when Kennedy entered office, Americans had spent 30 percent of the previous eight years in recession. This figure is so unusually large that it is difficult to find comparable periods in all of American history. For example, from 2000 to 2015, not a particularly good economic era, the economy was in recession for twenty-six months, or 14 percent of the time. From 1983 to 2000, the United States was in recession for all of eight months—4 percent of the time.

That the 1950s were not years of consistently expansive, ever-blooming prosperity is a surprise to many Americans, who are given to think that the first full decade after World War II was phenomenal economically, perhaps the greatest era of prosperity that there ever was. According to popular lore, in the 1950s jobs were abundant, they paid well, they were for life, you could raise a big family, afford a new suburban house, several cars, and then some.

It's true that the 1950s saw some notable expansions of prosperity. Suburbanization was in full swing. The number of single-family homes in the nation was in the process of increasing by eleven million over the decade, a jump of over a third. Televisions, appliances, and cigarettes were flying off the shelves. Spending on sports, recreation, and foreign travel was at high levels. By 1958, people were devoting a quarter more money to eating out than at the beginning of the decade. Advertising came into its own, accounting for $10 billion of the national economy, the same share as the market for new cars.

However, the prosperity of the 1950s was constantly interrupted, and was experienced by a shrinking share of the American people. From 1949 through 1960, the American economy fell into recession four times. Four recessions in eleven years—a dubious feat that the economy has accomplished only twice since 1929. (The other occasion was 1970–81, when Kennedy's economic policy was forsaken.) There was a recession in 1948–49, in which the ranks of the unemployed swelled to four million. There was a recession in 1953–54, in which unemployment again hit four million (with another half million giving up on work altogether). There was a recession in 1957–58, in which unemployment moved up past five million. And there was the recession that provided the context for John F. Kennedy's victorious campaign for president in 1960, the one that was still lingering as he asked the American people to "ask not what your country can do for you." In that recession, unemployment again hit five million.

Serial recession—a downturn every three years or less. This was the predicament of the American economy in the years in which Kennedy came of age as a politician, when he was a congressman, senator, and presidential candidate. If anything was clear to the preternaturally ambitious JFK in 1961, it was that if he wanted to make a difference as president in the 1960s, he had to identify and solve this problem—a reality he acknowledged more than implicitly in his own inaugural words. Serial recession had to stop in favor of uninterrupted growth. Otherwise, Kennedy would prove to be an ordinary, a status quo, a caretaker president. The Kennedy hype and "mystique" would all be for naught, a con job, cover for incompetence, if the fledgling young president could not "get this country moving forward again."

What was holding back the economy so persistently in the 1950s and early 1960s? The government was—by design, as hard as that may be to believe today. The income tax rates of the United States were enormously high during this period, far above anything we are familiar with today. The top rate of the federal income tax was 91 percent: no misprint, 100 minus 9 (today's top rate is about 40 percent). If you were a top earner, a member of the upper echelon of the "1 percent," as we say today, you had to fork over upwards of 91 cents for every dollar you made over a certain threshold.

It was not only the ultra-high incomes that had to deal with big tax rates. There were twenty-four levels, or "brackets," in the income tax code. Every time you made a little more money, your extra earnings— even if just for a cost-of-living increase to keep up with inflation— were taxed at the highest rate your income had been subject to before, or your raise threw you into an even higher tax bracket.

The first bracket hit a typical individual with a yearly income of $700 (some $5,600 today) with a rate of 20 percent (today's bottom rate is 10 percent). After that, rates increased a few percentage points with every few thousand dollars in further income, to 22, 26, 30 percent and on up, all the way to the final nosebleed rate of 91 percent, which affected those reporting income of over $400,000 per year.

Though the high rates might have been defensible when the government was desperate for money during World War II and the Korean War, in peacetime they served to stifle economic initiative and growth. Every time people started to earn more money, a greater portion of their income was siphoned away to the government. And every time they started to earn less money, their tax rates went down, meaning they got to keep a greater share of their income than before. Incentives in this code of "progressive" income tax rates were backward. Doing well came with proportionately lower take-home income, and doing poorly with tax relief.

When Republican Dwight Eisenhower ran for president in 1952, he indicated that he wanted tax rates to go down. They were plainly too high. He had a condition, however: spending had to fall first. The editorial page of the *Wall Street Journal* agreed with Ike. In a telling 1953 editorial, the *Journal* wrote, "General Eisenhower and [Republican] Senator [Robert A.] Taft [of Ohio], of course, have the right idea. The way to talk about tax reductions is to talk about spending reductions. So long as we have a $75–79 billion budget and a $5–10 billion deficit, it's a waste of time to talk about lower taxes. When we have a budget in balance tax reductions can follow automatically. You can't unlock the door with any other key." This remained the posture of the editorial page of the *Journal* (and many Republicans) on tax cuts under its editorship by Vermont Royster through the 1960s, including the era of the Kennedy tax cut. First spending cuts, then tax cuts. Or, as actually happened in the 1950s: no tax cuts, because spending cuts never came.[3]

There were moments in the early Eisenhower years when members of the administration considered tax cuts in the expectation of future spending declines. Eisenhower overruled such suggestions. Instead, he opted for accelerating federal spending, whereby programs already planned would be put in place sooner rather than later. In seeking to spur general economic activity by boosting government expenditures during a recession—the classic "Keynesian" alternative—Eisenhower guaranteed that he would never cut income tax rates. There would always be a deficit to take care of. Eisenhower himself had to quash the idea, floated by advisers, that he was intent on cutting taxes at some point in his administration. In a press conference in 1953, he said, "In spite of some things that I have seen in the papers over the past 8 or 9 months, I personally have never promised reduction in taxes. Never."[4]

The big progressive income tax code ensured the frequency of economic slowdowns in the postwar period. Economists at the time actually agreed on this point, arguing that the tax rates kept the economy on an even keel. The tax code's sharp progressivity was an "automatic stabilizer," a term coined in the 1940s, when income-taxes-for-everyone first came in.

The logic went like this: As people made more money during economic expansions, they were thrown into higher tax brackets, and the government collected a greater proportion of national income than before. The effect of the expansion was thereby dulled, a mild recession would hit, and people would fall into lower tax brackets as their income declined. This would amount to an effective tax cut, and an expansion would start anew.

Small boom and small bust, small boom and small bust, with inflation held off because the government was still guaranteeing foreigners the dollar for $35 per ounce of gold, as arranged at the Bretton Woods monetary conference in New Hampshire in 1944. This was the mild course that the economy was on, thanks to progressive taxation and the slim link to gold in the Eisenhower years. It was, in theory at least, a way to ward off both runaway booms, with their inflation and shortages, and depressions, with their inhuman levels of unemployment.

Three things were clearly wrong with this state of affairs. The first was that recessions were too frequent. That of 1960 was the fourth in eleven years. They were coming so often that not all of those laid off in one recession could find a job by the time the next one hit. The "structurally unemployed" were a growing group.

The second problem was the long-term growth rate around which the booms and busts occurred. From the 1953 economic peak to the trough at the end of 1960, namely the Eisenhower economy left at JFK's doorstep, the national growth rate was a mediocre 2.3 percent per year, barely clearing the population growth rate of 1.7 percent. From the 1957 economic peak through 1960, the private sector grew at 1.5 percent per year, while government grew at 4.3 percent. With any persistence of these trends, the postwar prosperity that the nation had begun to develop since World War II had no hope of being maintained, let alone enhanced.

The third problem with the "stabilization" brought by high tax rates was that it really benefited only the already affluent. Often, the very richest Americans supported maintaining the high tax rates, not because these rates were means of making useful contributions to the government, but because it was easy for the wealthy to find loopholes. A 1959 congressional study found that only about a fifth of those tippy-top earners who theoretically should be paying the 91 percent rate had declared income subject to that rate or those close to it. Typically, such earners paid an average rate of tax that was well below 50 percent.

A quick glance at the 1950s tax code reveals a problem. The entire code was about ten thousand pages in length. The first two pages were the list of rates, and virtually the whole of the remainder was devoted to statutes passed by Congress whereby individuals or businesses could dodge the regular 20 to 91 percent rates in favor of a total exemption or rates on alternative lower schedules in the back pages of the code.

Big corporations preferred such arrangements because they could afford to hire two kinds of specialists: lobbyists to get Congress to write pet tax exclusions into the law, and accountants and lawyers who could exploit the tax code to the company's advantage. Established companies knew that only the biggest, most moneyed, and most experienced firms had the resources and contacts to pursue this course. Start-ups that might threaten a big company's market did not have cash flow or the Washington, D.C., networks, putting them at a competitive disadvantage as they confronted progressive taxation.

Labor unions, for their part, disliked how corporations could pay their executives such that their compensation avoided high tax rates, necessitating further exactions from the little guy in order for the government to keep up revenue. Unions also detested what they referred to as the "swindle sheet," whereby business expenses ranging from country club dues to city apartments to yachts earmarked for corporate entertainment were excluded from taxation.

All the same, labor unions approved of certain effects of the sharply progressive income tax system. Along with the corporations, unions favored the way the code excluded certain kinds of worker compensation (such as health insurance) in the context of high tax rates. Workers would feel the pressure to join a union, because it took a union to negotiate such valuable compensation deals. Furthermore, unions did not really mind the slow rate of economic growth that accompanied progressive taxation. A lack of economic growth meant that jobs were scarce, raising the value of being a member of a union that had the muscle to negotiate who got hired with the big firms.

Inevitably, the joblessness of the 1950s fell primarily on those who were removed from the center of the corporation/union power nexus. Youth unemployment built up steadily from the 1948 low point of about 6 percent, hitting 18 percent in the summer of 1958. Ominously, the increasing difficulty teenagers were having in finding a job was occurring while the members of the baby boom were still young children. If the nation did not solve this problem soon, the numbers could become startlingly large.

African Americans bore the brunt of the recessions more than any other group. Black unemployment was consistently double that of whites. When unemployment crossed 7 percent in the nation in 1958, it crossed 14 percent for blacks. Certain unions conspired to exclude blacks from membership and from skilled trades, leading to blanket absences of African Americans in major union-organized industries, such as in the brewing and transportation of beer in Los Angeles. What equality in misery that did exist was small comfort; as one black newspaper headline testified as the economic downturn intensified in February 1958, "Color Line Fades in Memphis as Recession Revives Bread Line."[5]

As the rich profited and union members worked, and while structural unemployment worsened, newcomers to the workforce and disfavored minorities could not land a job, and the economy grew increasingly slowly, poverty began to become a formidable problem in America. *Commentary* magazine took the lead in exhibiting the intensifying travails of the poor and marginalized. A story on the effects of the 1957–58 recession in Gary, Indiana, found that "because those with the least seniority are laid off first, the most recent arrivals to Gary—Negroes, Mexicans, Puerto Ricans, 'hillbillies'—and the youngest members of the workforce generally, have so far borne the brunt of the cutbacks." The story added, "If there is one pervasive symptom of the economic situation, it is the almost compulsive way in which people keep referring to the depression of the 30's."[6]

In 1959, *Commentary* followed up this reporting by commissioning a young New York social worker named Michael Harrington to investigate the claim that America was developing into *The Affluent Society*, as in the title of Harvard economist John Kenneth Galbraith's 1958 bestseller. In an article titled "Our Fifty Million Poor: The Forgotten Men of the Affluent Society," Harrington dismissed the "current myth about poverty in the United States." This myth, stoked by Galbraith in his book, was that "the poor are a rapidly declining group." Harrington found that "as many as 50 million Americans continue to live below those standards which we have been taught to regard as the decent minimums for food, housing, clothing, and health." And he pointed out that "in the last two years, the numbers of the poor have increased; and some of the progress made previously toward minimum standards has been wiped out. Those who were already poor were the first to become unemployed in the recession of 1958." As it would during the recession of 2008–9, Detroit provided the starkest example of the devastation wreaked by recessions. In early 1958, sales of cars and trucks were down more than 25 percent from their 1955 peak. Three hundred thousand automotive jobs had been lost. One in six workers in the Detroit metro area was out of work. In Michigan, the unemployment rate was 15 percent. As a newspaper profile presented it:

> Drive out Detroit's East Jefferson Avenue, the main thoroughfare to the well-kept suburb of Grosse Pointe, and in one five-mile stretch you see: More than 50 abandoned stores, lunch counters, barber shops and other small retail businesses—A line of patient applicants for relief shuffling toward the double doors of the ancient, castle-like Public Welfare Department Building—A neighborhood movie house hinting at its efforts to double as a cheap hotel with the announcement: "New Policy—now Open All Night"— A half-empty workers' parking lot just west of Chrysler Corp.'s main Chrysler division plant—A corner pawn shop with a disconsolate sign over its loan window that notes unapologetically: "No Funds for Loans Until Next Week."[7]

By any measure and assessment, America's economy was on an unfortunate course. And yet as the 1950s lurched from recession to small boom and back again, with the class of structurally unemployed and poor growing each time, the unwieldy consensus that kept tax rates high solidified. Republicans worried about balanced budgets stood fast at every opportunity to cut tax rates. Economists who preferred "automatic" economic stability, as opposed to a course of big boom and big bust (the apparent precedent of the Roaring '20s and depressed '30s of recent memory), endorsed progressive taxation. The

Fortune 500 (a list begun in 1955) traded an economic pie growing at a greater rate for protection from entrepreneurial competition. Unions played along with high tax rates, knowing that business owners were gaming them, because they pushed more workers into their arms.

The average American was feeling the slow burn of diminishing economic opportunity. Cultural markers showed that the great middle class of the United States was beginning to get worried. Sloan Wilson's *Man in the Gray Flannel Suit* of 1955, adapted into a movie starring Gregory Peck and Jennifer Jones the following year, exhibited the increasingly excruciating difficulty of getting by on a regular salary and avoiding the layoff cycle. If the washing machine had to be replaced, even repaired for a chunk of money, it was a crisis. Scour John Updike's *Rabbit, Run*, a fictional portrait of American life published four days after Kennedy's election, and you will find no sign of the vast and prosperous middle class reproved by Galbraith. Updike's well-populated world has a few well-heeled people, and most are getting by, but the mythical prosperity of the 1950s is conspicuously missing. Instead, it was not at all clear that prosperity, let alone affluence, was to be the lot of the nation going forward.

By the time Kennedy was elected, the number of persistently unemployed and economically marginal Americans numbered well into the eight figures, tens of millions of persons out of a population of 181 million in 1960. Kennedy knew his country well when he mentioned "poverty" and "poor" several times in his inaugural address. Exceptionally privileged as he was, he would not have been an observant or a responsible leader had he not taken stock of this great problem that had become attached to the American economy in the high-tax era.

It was clear enough that Kennedy understood that something fundamental was wrong with the American economy, and American leadership in the world economy, when he became president on January 20, 1961. The question that remained unanswered, as Kennedy left the rostrum after his stunning inaugural address, was precisely what he was going to do about it.

Chapter 2

PATH TO POWER

Handsome young John F. Kennedy seemed like an unlikely candidate to empathize with the poor and to introduce brilliant economic legislation. It's true, though little known today, that the Democratic Party had a long history of cutting taxes in its early years, but the party was drifting away from that position, and Kennedy certainly didn't seem to have strong opinions on the topic that would make him stand against the tendency of the day. The only hint that he would cut taxes came from his interest in history, an early curiosity that would eventually mature into strong policy.

In his first years in government, though, it was difficult to distinguish between his interest in history and his interest in an author of a book about that history. Years before he became president, one evening in the spring of 1953, Kennedy took Margaret Coit out for a date. While driving through D.C. in his convertible, the freshman senator remarked to his date, who had won the Pulitzer Prize two years before for her biography of the nineteenth-century South Carolina senator and vice president of the United States John C. Calhoun, "I would rather win a Pulitzer Prize than be president of the United States." Flattery? Possibly, but Kennedy's interest in history, and in Coit's subject in particular, seemed genuine, and his ambition certainly was. John F. Kennedy "was driven," Coit recalled as she thought about the incident thirteen years later, in 1966. "He was the most driven person I had ever seen in my life. We went by the White House, and . . . he said, 'Do you think I have the drive of Andrew Jackson?' All I thought was that he was kind of crazy. I think he frightened me more than the facts warranted. He just was a little out of my league."[1]

A few months after this encounter, in September 1953, Kennedy married Jacqueline Bouvier, and he probably saw Margaret Coit only one time after the marriage, when the two ran into each other at a

National Book Award event. But even as his interest in Coit faded, his
interest in Calhoun remained. Through the years of his presidency,
every time Kennedy was asked for a list of his favorite books, he included Coit's *John C. Calhoun: American Portrait* (1950).

Calhoun is known for his hatred of the "Tariff of Abominations"
of 1828. The tariff—the rather comprehensive tax that the United
States put on imported goods for more than a century—was the government's principal means of federal revenue from the ratification of
the Constitution in 1789 all the way until the adoption of the income
tax in 1913. So central was the tariff to the American tax system that
for one long run, from 1817 to 1861, it was the only federal tax at all.
When the Democratic Party first came into being, in the time of Calhoun, its main goal was to reduce the size and complexity of the tariff.

Though the Democrats of Kennedy's early years as a congressman
would be skeptical of rate cuts, the party did have a long-standing
tradition of cutting tax rates, thanks to Calhoun. The nineteenth-
century Democrats believed that cutting tax rates would, aside from
prompting economic growth and fairness, result in an increase in tax
receipts to the government. Calhoun and his Democratic supporters
in the cause of tariff reduction spoke repeatedly in the 1840s of the
"maximum point of revenue" that can be achieved by a lower rate of
tax. Today this is the concept behind the "Laffer curve," the supply-
sider graph (named after economist Arthur B. Laffer) showing along a
bell curve that tax receipts rise along with rates until a peak is reached,
after which they decline as rates rise further.[2]

Today the Laffer curve is embraced more by Republicans than by
Democrats, but when the Democratic Party came into existence in the
1820s, among its top priorities was the reduction of tax rates to as low
and even a level as possible, along with ridding the tax system of special provisions that the favored few had gotten written into law. Then
the party of the "common man," the Democrats knew instinctively
that high tax rates and tax complexity redound disproportionately to

the benefit of the rich and well-connected. A clean and unobtrusive tax system, along with a clear and reliable dollar, put everyone in the nation on the same footing before governmental economic policy. Americans would be free to pursue economic growth and opportunity, and the working classes would benefit as much as anyone else.

It was the Republican Party and its predecessor the Whig Party, in the nineteenth and well into the twentieth century, that argued that high tax rates, with clever exceptions here and there, coupled with government spending projects targeted at business infrastructure, made up appropriate economic policy. Treasury secretary Andrew W. Mellon shook up this consensus in the 1920s, when he convinced Republican presidents Warren G. Harding and Calvin Coolidge to cut tax rates substantially, but Eisenhower, in the 1950s, preferred to spend big money on highways and defense while keeping tax rates high so as to appear to be paying for everything. In one sense, the JFK tax cut that came in 1964 was an episode of the Democratic Party's expressing one of its founding positions: that the government is supposed to get out of the way, lest it set up preferences for the powerful and thereby squelch the general prosperity. But aside from his clear admiration for Calhoun, Kennedy at the time of his election did not seem eager to close loopholes and cut taxes. In fact, his background seemed likely to propel him in the opposite direction.

The young president, forty-three years of age in 1961, came from a family steeped in both the business of politics and the politics of business, but as a boy his career in either field did not seem particularly likely. His father, Joseph P. Kennedy, was a self-made businessman who had made most of his multimillion-dollar fortune in the 1920s as a movie distributor and producer and, during the first big downturn of the Great Depression—the Great Contraction—as a stock market manipulator and short-seller. In 1934, the forty-five-year-old Joe Kennedy accepted Franklin D. Roosevelt's offer to become the first head of the Securities and Exchange Commission (SEC), the federal agency created that year to rein in the very practices that had just made Kennedy a fortune on Wall Street.

The SEC's main reform under Kennedy was to require businesses to submit frequent reports about their financial wherewithal. The hope was that these reports would stave off misinformation campaigns on the stock exchange that could cause wild swings in stock prices and gaping arbitrage opportunities. Kennedy had been a specialist in these campaigns, particularly in the tactic of having agents repeatedly buy and sell to each other blocks of a particular stock in which he had invested. The impression would arise of market interest in the stock, other investors would take the bait and buy the stock in a bid to ride the hot issue, and Kennedy would sell into the strength and pocket the gain. He probably made in excess of $10 million (in dollars not adjusted for inflation) from these tactics in the 1920s and early 1930s.

John F. Kennedy was seventeen years of age, about to begin his senior year at boarding school at Choate in Connecticut, when his father got the SEC going in the summer of 1934. What career path would open for Jack was an unsettled question as he plodded through school. He had been doing poorly at Choate, failing French and Latin, and had to attend remedial summer sessions. He affected "careless indifference" in his assignments, as his older brother, Joe, wrote to his father at the beginning of Jack's junior year in 1933, adding, "It will be too bad if with the brains that he has he really doesn't go as far up the ladder as he should." The headmaster saw potential, if of an unconventional kind, in the younger Kennedy. To Joe Sr. he wrote, "Jack has a clever, individualist mind. It is a harder mind to put in a harness than Joe's." Jack might not be "as able academically as his high I.Q. might lead us to think. . . . I think we over-estimate Jack's present academic ability." Throughout school, Jack's favorite subject was history.[3]

It does not appear that through their prep and perhaps their college years, Joseph P. Kennedy dedicated himself to informing his sons of the ways of business. For one, Joe Sr. was away on business most of the time. In 1931, for example, he spent all of two weeks at home. In addition, his business practices were not the matter of friendly or delicate conversation. His methods in the stock market were animalistic. The biographer of *The Patriarch,* David Nasaw, put it this way: Joseph P. Kennedy "generated rumors, planted stories, spread gossip to drive prices up or down, depending on whether he was selling or buying. Rarely, if ever, did he hold on to a stock or bond very long. He preferred getting out with generous profits to waiting for windfalls." Joe Sr. conceded this himself: "The President appointed me chairman of the SEC because he knew that . . . I had studied pools [the misinformation operations] and participated in them and was aware of all the . . . trickeries of market manipulation. . . . I had engaged in many a furious financial fight and knew . . . when to duck and when to hit."[4]

When John F. Kennedy said, as president in 1962, that his father had "always told him that all businessmen are sons of bitches," his father's remark probably reflected an assessment of the real facts of how the Kennedy fortune had been amassed. Joseph P. Kennedy treated the arena of business as a form of open warfare, in which the point was to make large amounts of money with few qualms about whether another party in a transaction might be getting the shaft. Jack's first school of economics, or at least of business, was his singular family.

It is clear that the tremendous economic depression of the early 1930s scared Joseph P. Kennedy. He thought that the system might be crumbling from the kind of stresses that businessmen such as himself were putting on it. This indeed was his justification for jumping on the FDR bandwagon, launching the SEC, and outlawing his favorite trading practices. In 1936, he published a book called *I'm for Roosevelt,* which rehearsed these themes. At his Harvard reunion in 1936, his businessmen-festooned class was aghast to hear Kennedy say that he was all for organized labor.

As a result of that scare, Joe Sr. wanted his sons to know about so-
cialism and left-wing politics. On the advice of FDR adviser Felix
Frankfurter, he persuaded his oldest son, Joe Jr., to take a year before
Harvard to study in London with the socialist economist Harold
Laski, today remembered as the chief antagonist of free-market champion F. A. Hayek. Joe Jr. so enjoyed his year with Laski that Joe Sr.
suggested the same course of action to Jack. Jack went to England after
Choate, but he spent little time with Laski. Instead he socialized with
friends and eventually took ill and returned home.

Back in the states, Jack was a Rank Group IV student during his
first years at Harvard, placing him in the bottom third of the class. But
his topic of study pleased his father. Joe Sr. had wanted Joe Jr. to major
in economics at Harvard but was content when he chose government
over philosophy. By his senior year, 1939–40, Jack had settled, like his
brother, on a government major, and he wrote a thesis on the tumult
of British-German relations in the 1930s, just then about to culminate
in the Luftwaffe's blitz over London. Proud of his son's work, though
Laski called it "very immature," Joe Sr. had the thesis published (to
heavy sales) under the title *Why England Slept*.[5]

In the fall of 1940, at the age of twenty-three, Jack headed off to
Stanford, where he became the first future president of the United
States to enroll in business school (the second was George W. Bush).
He stayed one semester. Kennedy does not appear to have applied
himself in business school, registering perhaps for just one class and
prompting the dean to make inquiries during the semester as to his
whereabouts. By November, he had taken an apartment with the
movie actor Robert Stack in the Hollywood Hills, hundreds of miles
from campus. "Have become very fond of Stanford," as he wrote his
old Choate roommate Lem Billings that fall. "Everyone is very
friendly—the gals are quite attractive and it's a very good life."[6]

Kennedy was drafted into the military while he was at Stanford, in
October 1940. In 1942, he and his brother Joe went off to war. Joe was

killed in Europe, and Jack himself narrowly escaped death in the Pacific, as he saved a buddy after his *PT-109* was struck and sunk by a Japanese warship. After the war, the Kennedy political hopes centered on him as the oldest surviving son. With inordinate help from his father, whose assistance included big money and very savvy public relations support (shades of the pools that Joe Sr. had operated prior to 1934 and that made him such an expert to head the SEC), Jack won a seat in the House of Representatives in 1946. He represented a district in and around Boston.

Jack's campaign glided lightly on the issues; its emphasis was more on personal interaction with voters, particularly women, than policy choices. The campaign made clear that Kennedy was a war hero. One issue on which he did focus was national health care, which he advocated. The provision of and payment for health care had changed during the war. Corporations and labor unions lobbied for and won a special clause in the tax code that remains to this day the king of all loopholes. This is the tax deduction for health insurance premiums paid under employer-sponsored plans.

Wages were "controlled" during World War II—they could not be increased, by law, for fear of sparking inflation. Unions wanted the health insurance loophole so that they could negotiate further compensation for their workers within the restrictions of the law. The added benefit was that nonunion workers would not have the standing to negotiate health insurance coverage from their employers. Big companies liked it, in that small companies and start-ups could not take advantage of the deduction.

In his first term in Congress, in 1947–48, an income tax rate cut came up for vote a number of times. Kennedy always voted against it. This was a bill championed by Senator Robert A. Taft of Ohio—who would unsuccessfully seek the Republican nomination for president against Eisenhower in 1952. The bill sought to trim the huge World War II–era tax rates by upwards of 20 percent apiece. President Harry

S. Truman, a Democrat, pledged to veto the bill, a pledge he fulfilled three times. On the last occasion, in April 1948, the House and Senate overrode the veto. A watered-down income tax cut, with rates shorn by 5 to 13 percent, became law. Within a few years, under the pretext of the Korean War, the provisions of the Revenue Act of 1948 would be largely repealed. In the early 1950s, most rates of the income tax, including the top rate, churned back up to where they had been before 1948: twenty-four progressive rates running from 20 to 91 percent.

Why did JFK vote against the Taft tax cut that ultimately enjoyed supermajority congressional support? Probably because he did not want to alienate the president, the Democrat Truman. Kennedy was a cub representative in the House in 1947–48, a rookie, and Truman was the handpicked successor to FDR, who had made JFK's father's career as a public servant. In subsequent years, as he became a seasoned officeholder, Kennedy made no pretense of fondness for Truman, and Truman reciprocated the hostility. In 1960, Truman said that he preferred Hubert Humphrey for the party's nomination for president, and he rued the influence of Kennedy money in the campaign. In 1963, when Truman came out against JFK's tax cut, JFK laughed out loud at the news on national television.

Joining Kennedy in voting against the tax cut of 1948 were Democratic representatives Lyndon B. Johnson of Texas, who as president would sign Kennedy's tax cut bill in 1964, and John W. McCormack of Massachusetts, the Speaker of the House when that later tax cut passed. Democrats in favor included Representative Wilbur Mills of Arkansas, the chairman of the House Ways and Means Committee in 1963 who guided the Kennedy tax cut through the legislative process.

Kennedy showed little interest in the tax-cut debates, such as they were, of the 1950s. He witnessed these first in the House, through 1952, and then in the Senate, after he won the junior seat from Massachusetts that year, bucking the big Republican wave.

As a senator, Kennedy's main preoccupation was, initially,

history—as dictated by his health. In 1954 and 1955, after surgery for a chronic back condition, he had little choice but to stay at his Washington home or office all day long and recline, as opposed to working the floor and the cloakrooms at the Capitol. (When he met Coit on the date in 1953, every time he stood up and walked around, he had to use crutches.) He took advantage of his time stuck in a chair or on the couch by reading, writing, dictating, and talking on the phone. He made an academic fellowship of his first several years in the Senate, and out of it came *Profiles in Courage*, a portrait of leading lights of the U.S. Senate from over the years, in January 1956. With the assistance of Joseph Kennedy's influence on the prize committee, the next year the book collected the Pulitzer in biography, the same category as Coit's *Calhoun*.

Otherwise, Kennedy's interests in the Senate were in foreign affairs and rooting out corruption in the labor unions. In 1960, fresh off reelection to the Senate two years before, he opted to run for president. As he did so, the economic issue was forced upon him by the recession that hit that spring.

It was actually the Republicans who had started discussion of the problem of the anemic economic growth of recent years, as they jockeyed for position to succeed Eisenhower. Nelson Rockefeller, the Republican governor of New York, like JFK the favorite son of one of the nation's biggest fortunes, had lent his name to a national goal of 5 percent economic growth—double the Eisenhower-era average. In a much-discussed report of 1958 issued by Nelson and his brothers' family's foundation, the *Rockefeller Report* (as it was known colloquially) made the case that if economic growth could be 5 percent as opposed to 3 percent through 1967, the nation would be a fifth richer and able to afford all manner of public and private goods.

To achieve the goal of 5 percent economic growth, the *Rockefeller Report* recommended income tax rate reduction—exactly the thing on which Eisenhower had never budged. "Our tax system presents a series of important impediments to growth," said the report, adding that the "very high graduated rates in the personal income tax structure reduce the incentive . . . to accumulate capital and put it to productive use. . . . The nation would be better served by an income tax with somewhat lower rates." The one goal was paramount: "the promotion of growth."[7]

Nelson Rockefeller had his issue, should he decide to run for president. The incumbent vice president in 1960, Richard Nixon, who was dead set on running, was not in a favorable position to call for improved economic growth, much less tax rate cuts. He had been with Eisenhower all along, as the recessions kept coming and tax rates stayed high. Early in the 1960 campaign, Nixon waved off calls for economic growth as "growthmanship"—an old line of Truman's advisers who believed that government spending could boost the nation's output. When it became clear that the country was heading into yet another recession, Nixon sensed that he had to co-opt Rockefeller. He had to become a critic of the economic status quo, and thus dismiss a reason for Rockefeller to make a play for the nomination at the party convention. Nixon called for a meeting with the New York governor to assure him that he too was now an advocate of higher economic growth.

The meeting took place at Rockefeller's sumptuous New York residence in July 1960, shortly before the Republican National Convention that would nominate Nixon. The two men issued a statement after they met, listing thirteen points of agreement. The chief one was this: "The rate of our economic growth must, as promptly as possible, be accelerated by policies and programs stimulating our free enterprise system." It gave the number of 5 percent per year that Rockefeller had first publicized two years earlier. The press mocked Nixon and Rockefeller's joint statement as "the Compact of Fifth Avenue."[8]

The Democrats had anticipated this idea and turned it to their advantage. In their party platform, released earlier the same month, they called for the *Rockefeller Report* growth rate, while taking a dig at Eisenhower: "We Democrats believe that our economy can and must grow at an average rate of 5 percent annually, almost twice as fast as our average annual rate since 1953."

Kennedy had not made much of an issue of economic growth as he prevailed over Humphrey and other challengers in the primaries. His speeches in the economic realm were scattershot, and favorite themes included the need to raise the minimum wage and to spend money on education. By the time he accepted the Democratic nomination for president in July, a national consensus on the issue of economic growth had formed independently of him, as the major party statements indicated. This consensus was that in a country as impressive and ambitious as the United States, economic growth was absurdly low, and unleashing its potential had to be a top national priority irrespective of who won the election in November.

As the campaign against Nixon began in earnest that late summer, Kennedy tried out new lines, signaling that he was beginning to grasp the nature of the problem. Chief among these: he would "get this country moving again." Sometimes it was formulated as "start America moving again." Kennedy used this line and its cognates, which became the campaign's signatures, on the stump, in debates, and in television commercials. He probably said "a rising tide lifts all boats" as well, a line that speechwriter Ted Sorensen recalled Kennedy using often since he had first come to the Senate. Kennedy also said that America had to get out of its "rut." The complacent young senator was now waking up to the economic dangers America faced.

In September, Kennedy rolled out a stump speech on his new economic perspective. The theme was growth. The recurring line was "with a really healthy rate of economic growth . . . ," after which Kennedy would detail some new achievement that the nation could make if the growth rate jumped, including alleviating poverty, building schools, and enhancing national defense.

The stump speech trashed the current trend of economic growth, pointing out that at best it was averaging merely 2.5 percent per year, that in addition to four million unemployed there were another three million underemployed, that "lack of growth means . . . a weak and declining nation." Kennedy observed that other countries, including West Germany and Japan, were sustaining high rates of growth well after the post–World War II rebuilding surges. He also said that the economy of the Soviet Union was growing sharply, a falsehood peddled by his liberal economic advisers.

Kennedy diagnosed the problem ably enough in his economic stump speech of the stretch run of the 1960 campaign, but he remained evasive about solutions. The most concrete thing he said was that he would de-control the development of domestic energy sources. Otherwise he was vague, when not suggesting that government spending and cheap money from the Federal Reserve could get the economy moving.

He began to be pressed for specifics. At a televised question-and-answer session with the public in Seattle in September, audience member J. T. Hong put this question to the candidate: "Senator Kennedy, . . . how do you plan to obtain 5 percent economic growth without raising taxes?" The question had an interesting premise, namely the view that the current federal budget deficit had to be closed in order for the economy to grow, a course of action that re-quired a tax increase (the standard Eisenhower/Republican view of fiscal policy of the time).

Kennedy's response was to reject the premise. "Let me say that I don't believe that there is an intimate relationship between raising taxes and economic growth. In fact, under present conditions, I can imagine nothing more deflationary than to increase taxes" (the term "deflationary" in this context surely referred to economic growth as opposed to the price level). From there, JFK still declined to get into specifics. He went on to say that taxes were as yet not a central part of his message: "The only time I discussed them, would be if we had a[n] . . . emergency . . . and our economy was booming and we suffered a serious danger of inflation. . . . But if you are talking about economic growth, there is not an intimate relationship [with] a tax increase. In fact, in my opinion, they would be contradictory."[9]

The furthest Kennedy got in outlining his economic policy plan came in a succession of speeches in October. In a new speech aimed at business audiences, he did at last imply, on October 12, that he might be interested in tax rate cuts. He said that he wanted certain business taxes cut, namely by allowing greater deductions for equipment purchases (a perennial issue in Congress in the 1950s). Then one small additional line in the speech suggested something more: "Taxes affect not only revenue but also growth, and a new administration must review carefully but with imagination our entire tax policy to see that these objectives are being met." In saying "our entire tax policy," and in having been consistent in previous months that he had ruled out tax increases, Kennedy might have been tipping off that he was interested in income tax rate cuts.

On October 20, two weeks before the election, Nixon seized on the easy-money portion of Kennedy's economic stump speech, saying that his opponent would cause "a totally stupid and unnecessary gold crisis . . . which could have disastrous consequences not only for America but the entire free world." On Halloween, Kennedy rebutted Nixon's charge, saying, "If elected president, I shall not devalue the dollar from the present rate" (of $35 per ounce), and made his most comprehensive statement of his economic plans to date.

He did this by listing six things that he would do to stimulate the American economy and keep the dollar stable against gold. He would balance the budget, manipulate interest rates, coordinate fiscal and monetary policy, consult business and labor on wage-price controls, "develop tax policies which will stimulate economic growth," and strengthen the nation's human and material capital. The fifth item, again, could only have implied tax cuts, in that Kennedy had repeated that economic growth would bear sole responsibility for increasing federal revenues.

The race was close, but on November 8, Kennedy won the election. For the next three years, he often kept tucked in his pocket a piece of paper scrawled with the figure "118,574." This was the margin of his popular-vote victory over Nixon, two tenths of a percent of all votes cast.

The official beginning of the recession of 1960 is today dated in April of that year. But recessions are least painful at their outset, and grow in intensity, in that unemployment develops as recessions deepen and employers make the difficult decision to let workers go. It was not until the fall that the layoffs started to come in earnest.

It was not lost on the political class that this may have swayed the election. Sorensen noted in his memoir that "the votes of the newly unemployed workers alone in Illinois, New Jersey, Michigan, Minnesota, Missouri, and South Carolina were greater than Kennedy's margins in those states." Nixon campaign manager Robert Finch agreed in principle: "Conceding the worst on everything else," he said in an interview several years after the event, "we still would have won if 400,000 people had not become unemployed during the last thirty days of the campaign." Nixon himself, in his 1962 memoir *Six Crises*, came to a similar conclusion, confiding that in January 1960 economist Arthur Burns had warned him that "unless some decisive governmental action were taken, and taken soon, we were heading for another economic dip which would hit its low point just before the elections." Nixon continued, "Unfortunately, Arthur Burns turned out to be a good prophet. The bottom of the 1960 dip did come in October. . . . Jobless rolls increased by 452,000. All the speeches, television broadcasts, and precinct work in the world could not counteract that one hard fact."[10]

Still, even with the recession, Nixon almost won. In 1960, the nation was so inured to frequent downturns that almost half the electorate gave its vote to the representative of the administration in power.

Kennedy was lucky that the recession had not tarried a few months more before it came.

Nixon, for his part, had not consistently made clear throughout the campaign that he felt there was an economic growth problem in the nation. He kept getting defensive about the current administration's record. In the first televised debate with Kennedy in September, for example, he implied that growth was a nonissue. Under Eisenhower, he said, the nation experienced "the greatest expansion of the private sector of the economy that has ever been witnessed in an eight-year period. And that is growth. That is the growth that we are looking for." Nixon must have been using nominal, nonadjusted statistics, because his claim was not legitimate. For example 1921–29 had real, inflation-adjusted private-sector growth far higher than after 1952. Nixon did repeat, on the stump, that he understood that "individual enterprise" was the key to growth, but refrained from outlining policies that would bring that result.[11]

Kennedy had been clearer than Nixon on the need for growth, as the recession reached its trough just at election time. That proved just enough to deliver Kennedy the votes. When it came to the *way* to deliver growth, however, Kennedy had remained almost as evasive as Nixon. It was plain enough that he had ruled out raising taxes—and that he would firm up the dollar against gold. It was also plain enough that he felt that whatever policies (outside of tax increases) brought growth would also result in higher revenues for the government. All the same, as of his election victory in November 1960, Kennedy had repeatedly touted government spending programs and loose money from the Fed, as opposed to tax rate cuts, as policies he favored to boost growth. As president, he would have to dispense with the vagueness and decide whether or not he would walk in the footsteps of his shrewd forebearer Calhoun. Surely he would have to do so quickly, because recessions were now coming with increasing and dispiriting rapidity.

Chapter 3

ADVISERS

How John F. Kennedy made decisions as president is a topic that has captivated interpreters for half a century. Most common is the view that he followed the lead of impeccably intellectual advisers. According to this theory, JFK collected and absorbed the best possible ideas and went with the crème de la crème. The former First Lady Jacqueline was perhaps more responsible than anyone for the currency of this view. The weekend following the assassination in November 1963, she gave an interview in which she said that her husband had adored the popular Broadway musical of the time about the knights surrounding King Arthur of old, *Camelot*, especially the line (written by JFK's Choate and Harvard classmate Alan Jay Lerner), "Don't let it be forgot, that once there was a spot, for one brief shining moment that was known as Camelot." Jackie added, "There will be great presidents again, but there will never be another Camelot."[1]

"Camelot" has since gone down as the metaphor of choice to describe the inner workings of the Kennedy administration. Historian Robert Dallek (to a degree ironically) titled his 2013 book on Kennedy's relationship with his advisers *Camelot's Court*; David Halberstam (backhandedly) characterized JFK's foreign policy team as *The Best and the Brightest* in his book of 1972. And yet this image of a trusted circle of genius advisers is not quite accurate.

Without question, Kennedy took steps to cultivate the impression that intellectuals surrounded him. In 1959 and 1960 this was an intentional campaign tactic, to differentiate him from middlebrow Eisenhower and lowbrow Nixon and to capitalize on the reception of *Profiles in Courage*. In particular, Kennedy assembled advisers from the top universities, favoring his home state's giants, Harvard and the Massachusetts Institute of Technology. While it is one thing to have premier intellectuals and scholars make up the better part of a president's advisers, it is quite another for those advisers to form actual presidential policy.

In Kennedy's case, it seems that he may have been more pleased to be surrounded by advisers than to be advised by them. Kennedy was possessed of a supreme self-confidence—of a type that might be incompatible with outsourcing policy prescriptions to advisers, let alone those drawn from the not-so-real world of academia. Reporter Robert Novak saw the influence of the professors and intellectuals all around Kennedy as slight. Novak wrote in August 1960, "One of the braintrusters admits: 'Not one of us calls the tune for Kennedy in any of the really important fields—defense, foreign policy, economics, the farm problem. . . . The wife of a Kennedy braintruster puts it this way: 'The best way to get an intellectual on your side is to ask his opinion.'" Novak supposed that Kennedy was courting professors so as to secure those in his party who were nostalgic for the scholarly Adlai Stevenson, the Democratic nominee whom Eisenhower had defeated twice.[2]

Whether Novak was correct in this reading of JFK's strategy, what is clear is that Kennedy's advisers were not a united group. As Kennedy in November and December 1960 assembled the economic team that would advise and put proposals before him as president, he appears to have, consciously or not, adopted what we now call the Abraham Lincoln "team of rivals" concept. Certain advisers were intellectuals and scholars, of a clear liberal bent. Others were not intellectuals, but rather men of affairs and more market oriented. Kennedy put strong representatives of both types of personalities on his economic team. He apparently wanted to entertain a breadth of opinion, perspective, and worldly experience, so as to give his freedom of choice a maximum scope.

The rival groups were the officials at Treasury and those at the Council of Economic Advisers (CEA). Kennedy tapped C. Douglas Dillon, the Eisenhower State Department official and an immensely rich Wall Streeter, to lead Treasury. Dillon was the representative of the market: he was in favor of managing the gold standard well and overhauling the nation's fiscal and tax policy in the direction of cleanness, simplicity, and efficiency. For the CEA, Kennedy recruited top liberal economists from the universities. These were modern Keynesians who felt that government spending, high tax rates, and deficits were the path forward. To complicate matters, during the campaign, Kennedy had also put together two "task forces" that were to give him a panel of recommendations on economic policy prior to the inauguration. The membership of these task forces included neither Dillon nor the future members of the CEA.

Either something had to give as Kennedy loaded up on economic policy advice, or he could somehow try everything. As events unfolded, he rather recklessly opted for the latter course. Perhaps inspired by Franklin D. Roosevelt before him, Kennedy would prove "experimental." In economic policy, over the nearly three years of the administration beginning in January 1961, he would favor a particular policy suggestion, put it into practice, and see if it worked; he would then ride the policy until it failed or otherwise lost its usefulness, at which time he would feel free to switch out what he was doing for deeper thinking and an untried recommendation.

By choosing this latter course, Kennedy introduced a drama to his presidency, since the changing policies would greatly affect the economy. Furthermore, since he tried policy seriatim, it was never crystal clear who among his advisers should get the credit for the success, especially if it came late, after many things had been tried. After all, if success comes late, cannot the advocates of an early policy that appeared to fail claim that in the end it was vindicated? Does not fantastic economic growth validate everything that roughly preceded it? As JFK was fond of saying in other contexts, while "defeat is an orphan," success "has a thousand fathers." After the JFK tax cut of 1964 produced spectacular results, all of his advisers claimed it was their idea—only a small handful of them with any justification.

John F. Kennedy's nominee to be secretary of the treasury, Dillon (whose name JFK offered on December 16, 1960), was something of a mirror image of the president himself. Eight years older than Kennedy, Dillon was the grandson of an immigrant and grew up as his father was beginning to make a very large fortune on the stock market. He went to a supreme eastern prep school (Groton) and then Harvard, and during World War II was decorated for his service in the Pacific. (Dillon was a naval flag officer and flew "Black Cat" bombing missions.) When *Fortune* presented its first list of the richest Americans in 1957, Dillon's father appeared in the rank one below Kennedy's father. Joseph P. Kennedy was between the eighth and sixteenth richest Americans, worth perhaps $400 million, while Clarence Dillon was about the twenty-fifth richest, worth as much as Nelson and David Rockefeller individually, perhaps $200 million.[3]

The difference between Jack Kennedy and Douglas Dillon lay in their choice of careers. After his few months ogling California girls (his own report of his activities) at Stanford Business School in 1940, Jack showed no further interest in a career in business. His father had set up ample trusts for each of his children so as to forestall any necessity for such a thing; the Kennedys, the four boys certainly, were free, indeed encouraged, to enter politics as a vocation. Dillon's father, in contrast, bought his son a seat on the New York Stock Exchange as a college graduation gift in 1931. Before he was thirty, Douglas was vice president of his father's firm, the investment bank Dillon Read. When Eisenhower became president in 1953, he named Dillon ambassador to France, a country Dillon had become familiar with in business dealings and by way of pastimes in art collecting and the family's Château Haut-Brion winery. Several years later, Eisenhower promoted Dillon twice within the State Department, first to the department's top position pertaining to international monetary affairs, and then to undersecretary.

Dillon was, in a word, cut from different cloth than the other individuals who made up Kennedy's economic team. He was a man of affairs, a public servant, and a bon vivant of the highest echelon, not to mention a

Republican. Kennedy had nothing on him—not money, not culture, not pedigree, not political experience. Kennedy had the presidency, but as secretary of the treasury Dillon would assume the one office within the government long considered rather coequal to the presidency.

As historian Irving Bernstein once wrote of the context that led to Kennedy's appointment of Dillon, "The Treasury was so venerable, so bureaucratized, and so powerful that, as [one wag put it], even Pennsylvania Avenue was forced to make a 'symbolic detour' to get around it. It was, as well, closer to the White House than any other department. Though Kennedy knew an enormous number of people, he knew no one he thought qualified to head this formidable agency. . . . As presidents are inclined when faced with this dilemma, he turned to that shadowy power center . . . called 'the American Establishment.'"[4]

Kennedy had first met Dillon on the platform at the center of the Harvard commencement ceremonies of 1956. Senator Kennedy was there to receive an honorary degree, and the twenty-fifth reunion class had elected Dillon chief marshal of the ceremony. Over the next few years, the Kennedys and the Dillons socialized in Washington now and then, Jackie taking the initiative to see that the Dillons' daughter Joan was introduced to fitting and interesting young people in society.

The Republican Dillon had "contributed substantially," as he recalled it several years later, to Nixon's campaign in 1960. Several weeks after the election, Kennedy came to his home in Washington and asked for his views on two matters. The first was economic growth—Kennedy was impressed that Dillon had supported the Rockefellers' talking-up of a 5 percent growth rate in the 1950s. The second was the "balance of payments"—the difference between the dollars sent abroad to clear transactions and foreign currency sent to the United States for the same purpose, a matter about which Dillon was not merely an expert, but one of the government's main managers. Kennedy offered Dillon the secretariat of the treasury, and Dillon accepted. He would become one of three Republicans in Kennedy's extended cabinet. The others were Secretary of Defense Robert McNamara and National Security Adviser McGeorge Bundy.[5]

As for the Council of Economic Advisers, Kennedy assembled this group in the weeks after the November 1960 election. He sounded out a professor he had come to know, Paul Samuelson of MIT (later the first American to win the Nobel Prize in Economics, in 1970) to chair the group, but Samuelson demurred in favor of being an independent consultant to the president.

Samuelson was a small man with sharp ears who friends said looked like an owl. He had an acerbic wit and a legendary cocksureness, especially in matters of economics. He also had a massive output of writing, in journals and eventually a *Newsweek* column. His written word—in particular, that meant for nonscholarly consumption (including memos to the president)—was an exercise in hidden ambiguity. His declarative statements somehow always included outs that gave him the option of saying that people were misinterpreting him. These ambiguities had an effect, in that for decades now since the 1960s, it has been a commonplace to say that Samuelson was the one who talked Kennedy into opting for a big cut in income tax rates. This is odd not only because a careful look at the historical record does not support this claim but also because Samuelson's chief contribution in the field of economics, as JFK was getting to know him, was in making a case for the opposite course of action.

In his research work in the late 1950s and early 1960s, Samuelson helped wield the national consensus that the American economy was not growing enough in the postwar years. His widely discussed solution was to pursue a policy mix of high tax rates on the fiscal side and loose money from the Federal Reserve on the monetary side. He developed this plan jointly with a young Yale economist named James Tobin, who outlined it in a July 1960 *New Republic* article baldly titled "Growth Through Taxation." In the article, Tobin called for an "increase in personal income tax at all levels" and then put it in italics: *"Increased taxation is the price of growth."* Tobin accepted Kennedy's offer during the transition to join the CEA, ensuring that the views he and Samuelson had come to jointly would have force on that body.[6]

The Samuelson-Tobin logic went as follows: Loose money from the Fed would spark economic expansion, as low interest rates got businesses to add to their plant and hire more workers. High progressive tax rates would in turn absorb any excess money that came from the expansion, staving off inflation. Full employment would result from the loose money, and price stability from the high tax rates. In addition, as the economy grew in this way, there would be a swelling in government revenue because—crucially—the high progressive tax structure was kept. Growth-oriented public works projects in infrastructure and education could then be funded out of a budget surplus. Samuelson and Tobin called their three-tiered plan the "neoclassical" or the "Cambridge–New Haven" (after the towns of the two economists' universities) "synthesis." It was made up of three parts: loose money, high tax rates, and increased government spending.

Another close associate of Samuelson's, Robert Solow, a young MIT economist, joined the Kennedy CEA with Tobin's Yale protégé Arthur Okun as staff (or assistant) economists, "in all but name additional members," as Tobin recalled it. Solow had published his theory of how modern economies can grow at higher than prevailing rates a year before the 1958 *Rockefeller Report*. His theory proposed switching out current consumption in favor of (presumably government) investment, supporting the last element of the Samuelson-Tobin plan. It brought Solow the Nobel Prize in Economics in 1987.[7]

After JFK named Tobin as a member of the CEA, and Tobin brought Solow on as a staff economist, both of those economists ensured that Samuelson's views would be amply represented on the council. The second member JFK put on the CEA was Williams College professor Kermit Gordon, another Keynesian, and the third member and chair was the only non–East Coaster, Walter W. Heller of the University of Minnesota.

Walter Heller was an economist of uncommon communication skills and wit. He was known throughout the profession for being able both to write an economically rigorous memo that was fun to read and to chat with noneconomists in a beguiling fashion at a cocktail party—rare talents. JFK had heard of Heller during the policy debates of the 1950s, and as he got to know him, he clearly came to enjoy spending time and conversing with him. As CEA chair, Heller became, if not one of Kennedy's most trusted advisers, the one whom the president preferred to be with. Sometimes the two would meet several times a day, Heller gracefully striding his six-foot-three frame into the Oval Office and entertaining the president with his famous conversational élan.

Heller was a supporter of the Cambridge–New Haven synthesis. As the *Wall Street Journal* reported on his appointment, in December 1960, "An advocate of low interest rates and generally large budget surpluses has been offered the job as President-elect Kennedy's top economics adviser," large budget surpluses being another way of saying high tax rates. Heller was clear on this point. He had told Congress the year before that he wanted to switch to "a combination of . . . greater monetary availability coupled with . . . higher net surpluses, and hence higher tax rates, than we would otherwise have." Heller did advocate, in the case of a sharp recession, a small, temporary tax cut to jolt the economy back to life. But without question he was part of the Samuelson-Tobin-Solow bloc within the congealing JFK CEA, holding that the *current* income tax structure had to be preserved for the long term.[8]

Heller, Samuelson, Tobin, and Solow were all abundantly on record, as they either joined or stayed close to the Kennedy CEA in the 1960–61 transition, as being intolerant of the Eisenhower-era sluggishness, insisting that the American economy was performing well below its capacity. Kennedy was in accord with this view, as his campaign had shown. He had to have economic growth. That outcome—major growth during and on account of the JFK presidency, after the tepidness of the Ike era—was consistent with the Kennedy ambition. The only question, and lurking note of disagreement with the CEA's opposite numbers at Treasury, concerned the means to that end.

To supplement the wisdom of his designated treasury secretary and CEA members, Kennedy also received during the transition the reports of the economic policy task forces that he had set up during the campaign. (Nixon had mocked this move, suggesting that Kennedy was wrongly implying that the nation was in crisis.) These reports, which came in two weeks before the inaugural, presented Kennedy with conflicting advice that corresponded to the nascent Treasury-CEA divide.

The first of the task forces concerned taxation. It was chaired by another professor, Stanley S. Surrey of Harvard Law School. Surrey had made his name in the 1950s as a relentless scholar of the brazen ways in which rich people avoided paying the high income tax rates of the day. One notorious case Surrey had brought to light was of the Hollywood mogul Louis B. Mayer. In 1951, Mayer had influenced Congress, via strategic lobbying, such that a law was passed that exempted exactly the kind of income he was about to receive as his lump-sum payment from his movie studio upon his retirement. The loophole affected all of two taxpayers, Mayer and his associate. It enabled him to pay taxes at a 25 percent as opposed to a 91 percent rate on a $2.7 million windfall—a savings of some $1.75 million.

Surrey had been trotting out examples of this sort in the *Harvard Law Review,* which became in the middle 1950s something of a running journal of the daring loopholes with which Congress, care of the lobbying of the rich and well-connected, was stacking the tax code, making the top rates near 91 percent a series of dead letters. A 1955 *Review* article by law professor William L. Cary related a remark by a Washington lawyer: "What is the point of litigating a tax case when we can have the statute amended for the same outlay of time and money?" John F. Kennedy named Cary to his father's old post as SEC chair in 1961.[9]

In 1959, House Ways and Means chairman Wilbur Mills asked Surrey to help his committee study the connection between high tax rates, loopholes, and the problem of economic growth. Mills had been a longtime supporter of comprehensive tax rate cuts. In 1948, he had voted for the Taft tax cut that both JFK and LBJ had voted against. Mills was also impressed with research undertaken by the Joint Economic Committee (JEC) in 1954–55 that showed that cutting tax rates in exchange for loophole closing could lead to economic growth on the order of 50 percent a decade—near the mythical 5 percent per year soon to be set as the benchmark by the *Rockefeller Report*.

Mills recruited a staffer from the JEC, a University of Chicago–trained economist named Norman B. Ture, to assist Surrey, while Mills arranged for congressional testimony on the subject. The proceedings filled a *Tax Revision Compendium* that ran twenty-four hundred pages. Surrey wrote the introductory essay and set the scene. The top rates of the income tax, Surrey reported, were doing next to nothing to collect revenue. Indeed, their primary function appeared to be, in practice, the diversion of entrepreneurial capital to tax shelters. Here was the root of the economic growth crisis.

Surrey's numbers were remarkable. He found that the average income tax rate paid by those making over $100,000—or the top .05 percent of all earners—was 36 percent, not 67 percent (the rate applicable at $100,000 in yearly income) or all the rates beyond that maxing out at 91 percent. The reason was not merely deductions, but provisions in the code that enabled vast amounts of income, particularly of the well-off, not to be reported. Surrey calculated that every year, less than half, about 43 percent, of actual individual income counted as taxable income—the rest was exempt, such as income from bonds of increasingly bloated state and local governments.

In addition, Surrey introduced a number, like the 5 percent per year growth proposed by the Rockefellers, fated to be a JFK-era benchmark: "A determined Treasury and a determined Congress could stop [these] trend[s]. . . . Any significant accomplishment in this direction as far as the upper bracket taxpayers are concerned would require a reduction in the top rates to 70 percent or 65 percent. The combination of such a reduction and the elimination of upper bracket [loopholes] would not necessitate a revenue loss." This was the number— a top rate of 65 or 70 percent, and entailing no loss in governmental receipts, proposed in 1959 (and mentioned by Surrey in his scholarly work prior to that)—that would organize the tax conversation of the Kennedy years.[10]

All these findings had made Surrey's reputation and prompted Kennedy during the campaign to have him chair his taxation task force. Surrey was assisted by Ture and three other tax lawyers. On January 9, 1961, in Kennedy's presence at the Cambridge, Massachusetts, home of Arthur Schlesinger Jr., Surrey delivered his report. It reiterated the findings of 1959. Income tax rates had to be cut, and as many preferences as possible closed. The report was technically silent about how low rates had to go, but it showed how easy it would be to reduce the top rates. It noted that while a one-point cut in the bottom rate of 20 percent would result in $1.5 billion less revenue to the government, taking the 91 percent rate down to 65 percent would cost a fifth of that, all of $300 million, and to 50 percent $800 million. There were so many exemptions from high rates, of the Louis B. Mayer variety, that "for many taxpayers, these steep rates are only paper rates." The report warned that a "program of tax reform necessarily arrays in opposition to it a variety of special pressure groups," namely unions, lobbying-inclined high-end individuals, and big, settled corporations.[11]

The taxation task force urged Kennedy to use the bully pulpit to inform Americans of how distorted the tax code had become, how beneficial a comprehensive rate cut could be for a nation surely disposed to a fair, simple, and modest tax system—and, crucially, how such a tax cut could unlock the potential for economic growth that had been stifled in the country for most of the decade and a half since World War II. The task force told him to press the issue himself in his own speeches and negotiations with policymakers and "pressure groups" and to get Congress to hold prominent hearings on the issue. Given that all this would amount to a major undertaking, the task force recommended that Kennedy submit his legislation in his second year of office, 1962. The first year would be spent preparing Congress and the special interests for the impending tax reform.

There was, of course, the possibility that the economy would persist in its 1960 sluggishness through 1961. In view of this, the report encouraged Kennedy, if he so desired, to seek congressional authority for a temporary tax cut lasting until late 1961 or early 1962. The thinking was that the recovery from the 1960 recession would have to be kept up at a decent clip for Kennedy's economic agenda to remain viable in Congress. A quick, expiring tax cut could stave off reversion to negative economic growth and to spikes in unemployment until the real tax-cut legislation came.

In all, the positions that Surrey's report laid out—how high tax rates redound to the benefit of the well-connected, do next to nothing to collect revenue, and lend a dizzying complexity to the law, all necessitating rather brutal impositions on the little guy—were true to Democratic traditions. They laid the tax perspective central to the founding of the party early in the century before on Kennedy's doorstep. After Kennedy got this report, Douglas Dillon tapped Surrey to be his assistant secretary for tax policy in the Treasury Department.

The second economics task force, on anti-recession measures, made its report in the first week of the new year of 1961. It was effectively a committee of one, Paul Samuelson, in that Samuelson wrote the report (while consulting with the CEA nominees) and delivered it personally to the president-elect at a meeting at JFK's favorite crash pad, the Carlyle Hotel in New York.

Samuelson's report differed considerably from Surrey's. It contended that a small, temporary tax cut (of no more than a 4 percent trimming of tax rates), along with a slew of targeted government spending projects, was necessary to sustain economic recovery in the administration's first year. And contra the taxation report, it suggested that the current tax rate structure would be good to keep around on a permanent basis, on the grounds that when the economy booms, it could reel in the revenue.

As for the spending, Samuelson really meant it. He said that the recession could be slipped if spending were accelerated in some dozen areas in 1961. There should be boosts in post office construction, teachers' salaries, water and highway projects, "depressed area programs" (as suggested by Senator Paul Douglas, Democrat of Illinois, Congress's resident Keynesian), slum clearance, national park recreational facility budgets, and military base building, among other things. With big money dedicated to government projects, the economy would rise out of the lingering recession and keep the new administration in the good graces of Congress and the American people. President Barack Obama's public works stimulus program of early 2009 was eerily similar to the Samuelson plan of early 1961.[12]

If his advice were taken, Samuelson wrote, there would be no need to do anything long-term when it came to taxes. "With new public programs coming up in the years ahead, sound finance may require a maintenance of our present tax structure, and any weakening of it in order to fight a recession might be tragic." Samuelson suggested that had his ideas along these lines been adopted several years before, the economy would now be 10 percent bigger. "Instead of our having now to debate about the size of the budget deficit to be associated with a recession, such an outcome would have produced tax revenues under our current tax structure sufficient to lead to a surplus of around ten billion dollars; and the authorities might be facing the not unpleasant task of how to deal with such a surplus."

By "deal with," Samuelson had already indicated that he meant "new public programs," not tax rate cuts or tax reform, whatever his rhetorical outs characterizing his opposition to permanent tax cuts as only pertaining to those that arose to fight recession. Samuelson was boxing out the Surrey report in favor of the Cambridge–New Haven synthesis.

Turning to the other half of the policy mix, Samuelson challenged Kennedy's repeated campaign promise not to devalue the dollar. *"It would be unthinkable for a present-day American government* [Samuelson put it in underscore] *to deliberately countenance high unemployment as a mechanism for adjusting to the balance of payments deficit. . . .* It is equally unthinkable that a responsible Administration can give up its militant efforts toward domestic recovery because of the very limitations imposed on it by the international situation." The idea that a dollar convertible in gold at its current set price of $35 per ounce, Kennedy's stated preference, was incompatible with robust economic recovery was Samuelson's assumption.

The office of the press secretary of the president-elect fired off the Samuelson report in a release. The full text appeared in the major newspapers. The taxation report remained unreleased and confidential. How Kennedy himself was weighing his economic policy options was not at the moment clear. One thing should have been obvious: neither Surrey nor Samuelson was a major adviser to the president-elect, nor were they set to be powerful members of the new administration. For these roles there would be Douglas Dillon at Treasury and Walter Heller at the CEA.

The press immediately picked up on the fact that there might be some tension on Kennedy's economic team, given Dillon's background and inclinations, the promises of the campaign, and the perspectives of the other advisers. As the *Wall Street Journal* put it the day after JFK tapped Dillon for Treasury, "America's economic future hangs heavily on one question: How will life be for Douglas Dillon, the lone Nixon Republican in the Democratic Kennedy cabinet?"[13]

The Surrey report had not been made public. Thus, as far as anyone could tell, as of early January 1961, the JFK policy mix was going to be loose money and government spending (with the possibility of a small, temporary tax cut), to solve not only recession but also the long-term economic growth problem. A defender of gold and prudent budgets like Dillon would be the odd man out. And yet clearly he was the top figure—he was the treasury secretary.

Kennedy liked the sense of disorder in his ranks, as his supreme biographer Richard Reeves would assess it in his book *President Kennedy: Profile of Power*: "The Kennedy I found . . . had a certain love for chaos, the kind that kept other men off-balance." Surely Kennedy would not let Samuelson be a persistent guiding light to him, in that Samuelson had no position in the government, and especially if he had rebuffed JFK on the CEA chairmanship. The CEA, for its part, had been in existence for only fifteen years. Its main responsibility to date had not been in establishing economic policy for the president, but in the subsidiary task of crunching numbers and statistics. Moreover, Samuelson and the CEA members were not worldly men of affairs (which is to say, the kind of man that Kennedy was), but impecunious professors.[14]

There is no doubt that the CEA advisers influenced Kennedy to some extent. He met frequently with his CEA, Heller in particular, and he visited with Samuelson in Massachusetts and Washington during both the campaign and the presidency. The logs and the presidential recordings verify the point. Not that the meetings were unfailingly professional. A naked JFK would summon Heller to the White House pool for a consultation. Kennedy charged John Kenneth Galbraith, Harvard professor and author of *The Affluent Society*, with playing the beard and squiring around Angie Dickinson, with whom the president had been having a torrid affair. This was to the great displeasure of the First Lady, in that Galbraith was one of Jackie's favorite confidants, not to mention an economic adviser to the president and an ambassador.

This was of a piece with how Kennedy had treated his professorial advisers in general. Harvard historian Arthur Schlesinger Jr., special assistant to the president, was the most loyal of this set, as evidenced by his fawning memoir *A Thousand Days* (1965). Schlesinger was, physically and personally, the picture of the intellectual egghead. Kennedy did things like give Schlesinger the chance to cavort with Marilyn Monroe when she was stuffed into one of her flesh-toned, body-hugging dresses at a party. Schlesinger responded to such sport in the fashion of the office square who puts a lampshade on his head. He got to be so frisky at administration soirees that at one point he followed the president's sister-in-law, Ethel Kennedy, in jumping into a swimming pool fully clothed.[15]

Kennedy appears to have treated all of the professors in particular in classic rich-kid, prankster fashion. He brought them into the center of power and then set them up as pawns in playful if not impudent social circumstances, and probably got a kick out of the whole thing while thinking he was being generous to them. To be sure, Kennedy did not keep professors around only for such diverting and superficial purposes—he did collect their advice. But the notes of mischievousness were there. On the matter of the tax cut, events would make plain that Kennedy came to the decision to favor it *against* the preferences of the economics professors on his team.

Douglas Dillon, in contrast, was a man more to Kennedy's taste, who had bestridden the global stage for three decades as a captain of finance and political economy. When Dillon made the move in January, when the presidential transition was winding up, to place Stanley Surrey highly within his department, he signaled his approval of a major reduction in income tax rates. The lines were being drawn. The Treasury would be the advocate of a big tax reform and a sound, gold-credible dollar. The CEA would carry the banner of loose money, the old progressive tax structure, and spending. And Kennedy would do as he pleased.

Chapter 4

A KEYNESIAN
FIRST YEAR

JFK's first two and a half months in office were free of major crises, a presidential honeymoon during which he would devote his attention to fixing the underperforming economy. In the spring, a trifecta of events hit that would focus administration attention away from economics and onto foreign affairs and civil rights: the botched Bay of Pigs invasion in Cuba and the Soviet Union's launch of manned spacecraft in April, and the torching of the Freedom Rider buses in Alabama in May. But before those events, Kennedy had time to communicate clearly his early economic ideas—and it's obvious that the CEA was winning him over in terms of tax and spending policy, and soon enough in monetary policy as well.

Right away, Kennedy was explicit about one way he was maintaining his campaign promises. At his first press conference, five days into his presidency, he dispelled any notion that he was wavering on the dollar. He said of his economic advisers, surely those at Treasury and explicitly not including Samuelson, "I will say that our study so far has convinced us that the dollar must be protected, that the dollar can be protected at its present value."

Five days after that, at his State of the Union address, Kennedy went further than he had in the campaign, characterizing the economy in extended remarks as in dangerously poor condition. "The present state of our economy is disturbing," he said as he began the substantive portion of his address before both houses of Congress. "We take office in the wake of seven months of recession, three and one-half years of slack, seven years of diminished economic growth, and nine years of falling farm income. Business bankruptcies have reached their highest level since the Great Depression. . . . Save for a brief period in 1958, insured unemployment is at the highest peak in our history. . . . Nearly one-eighth of those who are without jobs live almost without hope. . . . The rest include new school graduates unable to use their talents, farmers forced to give up their part-time jobs which helped balance their family budgets, skilled, and unskilled workers laid off in such important industries as metals, machinery, automobiles and apparel."

He continued, "Our recovery from the 1958 recession . . . was anemic and incomplete. Our Gross National Product never regained its full potential. Unemployment never returned to normal levels. Maximum use of our national industrial capacity was never restored. . . . In short, the American economy is in trouble. The most resourceful industrialized country on earth ranks among the last in the rate of economic growth."

Kennedy had not gone on in such a mordant vein during the campaign because the latest recession was only starting. By early 1961, the depth of the problem had been fully revealed. Kennedy spelled this out: "Since last spring our economic growth rate has actually receded. Business investment is in a decline. Profits have fallen below predicted levels. Construction is off. A million unsold automobiles are in inventory. Fewer people are working—and the average work week has shrunk well below 40 hours. Yet prices have continued to rise—so that now too many Americans have less to spend for items that cost more to buy."

It was grim, even bleak stuff. Then again, the reason that Kennedy had given the nation for running for president in the first place, at least once the growth crisis became a clear national issue during the campaign the previous summer, was that a collection of economic maladies of the sort he was now describing was coming on the scene. America was becoming "dangerously weak," as JFK had said on the campaign trail, and he would get the country out of its "rut."

But during the campaign, JFK had been notorious for not saying how. "Kennedy Asks Faster Economic Growth, but Offers No Specific Goal or Method," a press headline had aptly put it back in September.

Now that he was president, he had to say how. And in this first moment of truth, at the end of January 1961, he breathed barely a word about tax cuts. He offered big-time spending—one of the major components of the Samuelson plan.[1]

The list came fast and furious: "I will propose to the Congress within the next fourteen days measures to improve unemployment compensation . . . to provide more food for the families of the unemployed . . . to redevelop our areas of chronic labor surplus, to expand the services of the U.S. Employment Offices, to stimulate housing and construction, to secure more purchasing power for our lowest paid workers by raising and expanding the minimum wage, to offer tax incentives for sound plant investment"—the only mention of any kind of a tax cut—"to increase the development of our natural resources, to encourage price stability, and to take other steps aimed at insuring a prompt recovery and paving the way for increased long-range growth."

Kennedy added, "This is not a partisan program concentrating on our weaknesses—it is, I hope, a national program to realize our national strength." Indeed it was not a partisan program. Eisenhower had been battling recession from 1954 on by one major method: increasing transportation and military spending in the hope that by virtue of it, the economy as a whole would grow faster.

Kennedy was not done. "For our national household is cluttered with unfinished and neglected tasks," he said. "Our cities are being engulfed in squalor. . . . A new housing program under a new Housing and Urban Affairs Department will be needed this year. . . . Federal grants for both higher and public school education can no longer be delayed. . . . Measures to provide health care for the aged under Social Security, and to increase the supply of both facilities and personnel, must be undertaken this year. . . . A host of problems and projects in all fifty States, though not possible to include in this Message, deserves—and will receive—the attention of both the Congress and the Executive Branch. On most of these matters, messages will be sent to the Congress within the next two weeks."

Then Kennedy was off on the perils of the international situation for the rest of the address, in that, as he said, "all these problems pale when placed beside those which confront us around the world," referring to Soviet communism and so forth. To be sure, he was on the mark when he lamented the current condition of the economy. The official end, which means the worst point, or the "trough," of the recession that had lasted through and beyond 1960, we now reckon as February 1961. Unemployment, however, is what economists call a "lagging indicator," typically continuing to rise even after a recession reaches its bottom. Up it bounded in 1961, past 6.5 percent as Kennedy became president, on its way to 7 percent by April.

When it came to a set of actions for what to do about all this, the State of the Union offered a contradictory note to the signature line of the inaugural address of ten days prior. "Ask not what your country can do for you," Kennedy had said on January 20. On January 30, he gave the country a list of what it would be doing for the millions caught in the recession's tow. Spending, not a tax rate cut characterized by the incentive effect, was the policy on offer.

Aside from the State of the Union, Kennedy made two major statements on economic policy during his honeymoon, both in the form of special messages to Congress. The first, on February 2, fleshed out his pledge in the State of the Union to spend government money to get the economy out of recession. The second, on April 20, made the case that the United States had to reform its tax code. The two statements presented, implicitly, the two visions of economic policy put forward earlier by the task force reports. The February 2 message adopted the spending recommendations of the Samuelson report, and that of April 20, the tax program of the Surrey report. Kennedy made plain that he would do the one thing, spend the government's money, right away, but needed time for the second. He would get all sorts of projects funded right then, in 1961, so that the recession would depart. But the planning necessary for tax reform, and setting the stage for long-term economic growth, was too extensive for any legislation to be readied before his second year in office.

Why would tax reform take so long? It would seem that the major preparation and groundwork in Congress had already been done. Six years before, the Joint Economic Committee had floated the idea of major rate cuts in the context of loophole-closing. Two years before, the House's most powerful (and relevant) committee, Ways and Means, had taken twenty-four hundred pages of testimony resulting in the finding that there should be a 30 percent across-the-board cut in tax rates, beginning at the top, along with loophole-closing. Surrey's task force had done its work in 1960. Why not get a bill out there so as to forestall the potentially wasteful government spending programs?

In his task force report, Surrey had warned Kennedy about "pressure groups" that the new administration would have to win over or silence on the matter of tax reform. In fact, Surrey had suggested that Kennedy might have to take his whole first year as president softening up those groups before he introduced a bill. Hence Surrey's recommendation, at New Year's 1961, that Kennedy might have to take some temporary antirecession measures, such as a small expiring tax cut, to keep recession at bay, until the growth-enhancing big, permanent marginal tax cut came.

The "pressure groups" Surrey was speaking of were presumably the individual and corporate players and their lobbyists (the K Street crowd, as we say today) who thrived under the high-tax-rate/extensive-loophole system. Just as Surrey had feared, their influence was felt immediately on Kennedy's assumption of office. Wasting no time or efficiency, they went directly after . . . Surrey himself. Kennedy and Dillon had the devil's time that winter and early spring of 1961 even getting him—a Harvard law professor with extensive policy

experience in his field—confirmed by Congress for his junior appointment at Treasury.

The Surrey nomination, to be Dillon's assistant secretary of the
treasury for tax policy, brought out the surliness in Congress. Certain
members felt that he was a manifest insult to the body, in that his purpose in life appeared to be making public the vile ways in which the
rich and connected cowed representatives and senators into writing
tax preferences for them. Senator Harry Byrd of Virginia (who would
fight JFK's tax cut fiercely in 1963 until LBJ finally turned him in 1964)
accused Surrey in his appointment hearing of "not having a very high
opinion of Congress. . . . You think these tax laws were sneaked
through Congress without knowledge of a great many Congressmen."
Byrd was being coy. Of course Surrey's view was that the Louis B.
Mayer exemption and all the rest had always gotten through *with* the
knowledge of a great many congressmen.[2]

Surrey got Senate confirmation in April 1961, months after Kennedy had to lay out all his recession-fighting policies, and only after
Dillon had assured Byrd in writing that he, not Surrey, would have
final say on all tax policy coming from Treasury. A few weeks later,
with Surrey at last in place, Kennedy gave his speech informing the
nation that he was working on a package of comprehensive tax reform
that would include a significant reduction in tax rates. Surrey had his
task, now that he was allowed to occupy an office in Treasury. "I am
directing the Secretary of the Treasury, building on recent tax studies
of the Congress [which had been supervised by Surrey], to undertake
the research and preparation of a comprehensive tax reform program
to be placed before the next session of the Congress," Kennedy said in
April 1961.

The full message Kennedy made that April was intriguing. It
showed that he was distinctly concerned that the tax system was
probably the root of the nation's economic growth problem, regardless
of whatever he had been saying about the need for more government

spending in previous weeks and months. In the message, he confirmed what had become increasingly apparent since FDR about the high-tax-rate system, namely that it was aimed more at the little guy than at the rich and well connected. (As Surrey and a colleague had put it in 1953, during World War II the income tax "changed its morning coat for overalls.") Kennedy wrote in the introduction to the document, "In meeting the demands of war [World War II] finance, the individual income tax moved from a selective tax imposed on the wealthy to the means by which the great majority of our citizens participates in paying for well over one-half of our total budget receipts." This reliance on the average American for tax revenue was concerning enough in its own right, but the bigger problem lay elsewhere. "So many taxpayers have become so preoccupied with so many tax-saving devices [and,] moreover, special provisions have developed into an increasing source of preferential treatment to various groups. . . . The uniform distribution of the tax burden is thereby disturbed and higher rates are made necessary by the narrowing of the tax base."[3]

Kennedy outlined a solution: "It will be a major aim of our tax reform program to reverse this process, by broadening the tax base and reconsidering the rate structure. The result should be a tax system that is more equitable, more efficient and more conducive to economic growth." A portion of the message, however, still concerned various tweaks of the tax code that could be accomplished piecemeal in short order, even things that constituted tax increases, such as greater tax withholding. The big reform, including rate reductions, Kennedy made clear, would require time and study (and probably the campaign against the pressure groups)—he suggested eight months' worth.

In the offing, Kennedy proved better than his word on the pledges of the State of the Union and the follow-up message of February 2. Before the summer of 1961 was out, he had secured an extension of unemployment benefits, an area redevelopment act that provided

grants for water and sewer infrastructure (fast-tracked if unemployment in the region was high), an interstate highway act authorizing
$30 billion while keeping the 4-cent gasoline tax intact (signed by JFK
on the fifth anniversary of Eisenhower's first highway measure), and
laws expanding Social Security benefits and housing assistance and
increasing the minimum wage.

All of these were acts of Congress, signed into law by Kennedy.
Journalist Theodore White would later marvel at this flurry of signed
bills, with thirty-three out of fifty-three Kennedy proposals passing
Congress in 1961, "How much new legislation was actually approved
and passed into law under Kennedy—more than at any other time
since the 1930s." The laws were just the half of it. By his own authority,
Kennedy also in 1961 had government agencies accelerate their construction projects and procurement plans, stepped up post office construction, sent out veterans' benefits ahead of schedule, had major
departments (including Defense) direct-spending to "labor surplus"
(i.e., high-unemployment) areas, launched a pilot food stamp program,
and increased price supports for farmers. There was no way the economy was going to tip back into recession—the government spending
commitments that Kennedy pushed through would prevent it.[4]

Kennedy's rhetoric extolling this spending stressed government
activism—"stimulus," as we would call it today. "The Federal Budget
can and should be made an instrument of prosperity and stability, not
a deterrent to recovery," as Kennedy told Congress on February 2. He
added, "The programs I am now proposing . . . are designed to fulfill
our responsibility to alleviate distress and speed recovery. . . . They
will sustain consumer spending and increase aggregate demand now
when the economy is slack. Many of these expenditures will automatically cease when high employment and production are restored."
These latter examples presumably were the unemployment compensation and the labor surplus area actions—the "automatic stabilizers."
Heller actually preferred the term "tranquilizers."[5]

The further spending programs would, however, be long lasting. "Other measures contained in this message propose necessary uses of national economic capacity and tax revenue for our long-range growth, and are essential even in the absence of a recession. They are proposed because the country needs them, can afford them, and would indeed be poorer without them." Highways and water projects, new post offices, slum clearance—these government projects would lift up the economy to a plane of growth that it could not reach of its own accord, per Solow's (if not Galbraith's of *The Affluent Society*) growth theory. "Public expenditures must provide services which contribute to the growth of potential output," as the CEA put it in one of its reports.[6]

Kennedy's words on all these matters came in written form. They were surely drafted by his speechwriters and advisers, probably the professors on his CEA. "Aggregate demand," "slack," "national economic capacity" (an equivalent of "potential output")—these were keywords of Samuelson, Heller, and the CEA. "Aggregate demand," a neologism of the 1930s, referred to the total amount of spending taking place in the economy. If it went up, businesses would invest more. "Slack," also a term new to economics in recent years, was the degree to which the "national economic capacity" went unmet. If the nation had X number of machines and Y number of workers willing to work Z number of hours, the capacity would be all those figures multiplied. Actual economic performance—"gross national product"—subtracted from that capacity was the slack. Kennedy's economists said that the problem in the 1950s to date was that the slack in the American economy was getting large.

The CEA spent the latter part of 1961 putting its theories for the president on paper, to be published in January 1962 as the *Economic Report of the President*. This is the report that President Obama's CEA chair Christina Romer and the economics establishment have to this day held up as the supreme example of economists conveying theory to power. (Romer in 2010 spoke of "the glory days of the CEA in the 1960s, when Robert Solow [was a] senior economist . . . and James Tobin was a member.") Here is the CEA in the ballyhooed report, reflecting on what the administration had gotten started in 1961: "The single most important stimulant to investment is the . . . full utilization of capacity. . . . Expected profit from investment is strongly influenced by the expected demand for the output that the new capital will help produce. . . . During periods of economic slack . . . many projects are foregone which would appear profitable under conditions of high demand." About a "permanent reduction in tax rates," the report was only cautionary: they "would [come] at the possible sacrifice of tax revenues which would be most desirable [for] government programs."[7]

In our own day, such themes strike a false note. Workers times hours times machines—what can this have to do with anything, when a technological innovation can comprehensively transform the way people conduct their affairs? Today we speak of the "gales of creative destruction" (a term coined in the 1940s by Austrian American economist Joseph Schumpeter) that upend economic organizations when a fantastic new device or way of doing business comes on the scene. The premise of the venture capital industry is that a small (often sub–$1 million) investment can generate economy-transforming results, if the entrepreneur is visionary enough. Surely when Peter Thiel made his $500,000 angel commitment to Facebook and Mark Zuckerberg in 2004, he did not base his decision on an estimation that the nation's economic capacity was underused (whatever that could mean). As for the point that "during periods of slack . . . many projects are foregone," it has long been clear that recessions are a good time to start a business. Not only are the odds of a future economic upswing reasonable during a business trough but entrepreneurs can readily assemble labor and capital in the service of their new idea during recessions, because so much is idle. The classic example is Andrew Carnegie, who acquired the assets of his steel firm in the wake of the Panic of 1873.

The record of the Kennedy administration in its first year, 1961, was Keynesian. Consistent with the thrust of British economist John Maynard Keynes's 1936 magnum opus, *The General Theory,* the federal government was going to solve serial recession by committing money to public projects. The post offices, the housing, the highways, the Social Security and minimum-wage bump ups, the labor surplus area procurements, and all the rest would serve two crucial purposes. First, they would increase purchases, the government's own and those receiving government checks, thus increasing business activity and employment, smothering the residual Eisenhower recession. Second, they would provide a platform for future economic activity. The highways and housing (and schools and medical and industrial research, also goosed by the 1961–62 federal budget) would enhance the capability of the economy to grow more. The population would be more mobile, sheltered, educated, and knowledgeable—primed for economic growth—because the government had spent money on ensuring such things. Or so the CEA's argument went.

Where was the treasury secretary as the Kennedy Keynesianism reigned in 1961? How was life "for Douglas Dillon, the lone Nixon Republican in the Democratic Kennedy cabinet," as a reporter had queried back at Dillon's nomination by JFK the previous December?

Given the assignments that Kennedy gave Dillon at Treasury in 1961 and early 1962, it is clear why the new president was interested in the services of this investment banker, diplomat, and high Eisenhower official. Whatever the growth issue facing the nation, JFK had a pressing short-term international financial problem to solve, and Dillon's first task was to get that done. The Treasury became a hive of activity under JFK in 1961 and early 1962. Treasury's given responsibility was to stem the foreign run on the dollar that had developed during the later Eisenhower years and the sequence of recessions in the United States. After that urgent problem was taken care of, if JFK's occasional remarks over the first year were to be believed, there could be a chance for tax reform.

In the quarter century following World War II, the United States had a major promise to keep when it came to foreigners and the dollar. The U.S. Treasury had to supply, on demand, an ounce of gold every time a foreign monetary authority, typically a foreign central bank, asked for it, in exchange for $35 (the price set by FDR in 1934). To qualify for the ounce of American gold at $35 on demand, foreign countries had to ensure that in the private markets their currencies did not trade above or below a fixed rate of exchange with the dollar. In the case of the West German mark, for example, if it continued to trade privately at 4.2 per dollar, the United States would give the Germans an ounce of gold for $35—anytime they asked for it. The idea, a perfectly sound one, was that the currencies of foreign countries would be as good and welcome, in their own market and worldwide, as the dollar if they consistently traded at a fixed rate of exchange to the dollar. This was particularly important to countries regarded with suspicion, such as a West Germany and Japan, only a few years removed from having been the hated aggressors in World War II.

The dollar, for its part, would be good in markets domestic and global for similar reasons. People would have confidence in the dollar not only because it was the currency of the largest economy and the representative of the superpower that bestrode the world but also because it could not be oversupplied or mismanaged, in that it was redeemable in gold—and the American stock of gold, while large, was finite. The dollar was on a gold-price rule. Other major currencies were tied to the dollar, making them effectively on a gold-price rule as well.

This arrangement, called Bretton Woods, after the monetary conference held at the New Hampshire resort of that name in 1944, was an attempt to modernize the old gold standard of the nineteenth century that had supervised the Industrial Revolution. Given that the United States had most of the world's gold after World War II, it was unreasonable to suppose that other countries could guarantee their currencies in gold. Here was a way for them to do it: foreign currencies were guaranteed in the dollar, which itself was exchangeable in gold.

Bretton Woods worked surpassingly well. The countries that worked hard at following it, including West Germany, Japan, France, and Italy, saw rates of economic growth so stunning in the 1950s that their booms became as fabled in-country as postwar prosperity in the United States. *Wirtschaftswunder*—"economic miracle"—the Germans called their rush into highly gainful economic activity in the 1950s; to the French, these were the first of "thirty glorious years."

The one country, oddly enough, that appeared to be indifferent to the Bretton Woods system was the United States. Throughout the 1950s, and in particular in the wake of the 1957–58 recession, other countries started piling up large dollar stockpiles and preferred not to use them to invest in dollar-denominated assets. These countries soon began to ask or talk about asking for gold in return from the United States. This was a signal to the United States that it was overproducing its currency.

Overproducing its currency? Under the "conservative" Eisenhower, money was "tight," JFK had said in the campaign, as Nixon agreed. Yes, it was overproducing, even in the 1950s. If the nation was not growing, then investments within it were not valuable—and foreigners would prefer to exchange the dollars they held for other currencies, to invest elsewhere around the globe. The growth problem had turned into a dollar-integrity problem. Dillon had to manage it, first as an underling in the Eisenhower State Department, and now as Kennedy's secretary of the treasury.

It was all these prospects that had prompted Kennedy to make his Halloween 1960 assurance that he would not "devalue" the dollar—which is to say, inform other countries that the United States was changing the terms of the original Bretton Woods deal and require some amount greater than $35 for an ounce of American gold. Kennedy did not want to do this, and not only because it would mean continuing the "dollar drain" of the Eisenhower years. He also surely knew that devaluation is an act that does not inspire confidence. It implies a government that wants to print money beyond what the economy can usefully absorb.

Dillon's charge as JFK's treasury secretary in 1961 and the first half of 1962 was to prevent an international monetary crisis. (JFK at times called him daily about it.) Dillon had to see to it that foreigners did not hit up the Treasury for so many ounces of gold at $35 per ounce that the United States could not meet the claims. He addressed the problem in various ways, gobbling up the greater part of his time and energy. The result of his efforts, by early 1962, came in perhaps a notch above futility.

One thing Dillon tried was to help organize a clever (if nefarious) little setup called the "London gold pool," whereby the United States strove to fix the private price of gold. The pool was stocked with American and British gold reserves and would sell anytime the market price nosed above $35 per ounce. Given that foreigners would appear at the Treasury en masse for gold at $35 per ounce (as per the Bretton Woods provision) should they be able to sell it on private markets above that price, the United States would now intervene on those markets to see that this never happened.

Dillon also coordinated Treasury activities with the Federal Reserve. The main effort in this regard was a program called "Operation Twist," named after the dance craze of the day. Here the Fed would strive to keep long-term interest rates low and short ones high. This is the inverse of what usually happens. If you pledge to keep money deposited in a bank for a long time, you get a higher rate of interest than on deposits pledged for ninety days. "Twisted" interest rates—long-term ones low, short-term ones high—are counterintuitive, but in the autumn of 1961 they materialized, in the name of solving the dollar problem. Foreigners, according to the theory, would be reluctant to cash dollars out of the bank so as to trade them for gold if those dollars were earning good interest at the bank. Meanwhile, low long-term loan rates would encourage investment, drawing more foreign dollars away from potential redemption in U.S. gold.[8]

How well did these stratagems pay off? In the three years after the recession hit in 1957, the Treasury had to surrender a fifth of its gold to foreigners, a yearly loss rate of 8 percent. After all the policies and programs in 1961 and early 1962—which did not include any kind of tax cut—that rate had slowed to 5 percent.

One further thing remained to be tried to improve the situation. The economy could *grow more* so that people would want to keep their dollars for investment in the United States, justifying all the printing of the currency that had been undertaken. Ultimately, this is the realization that would come to Dillon—and to JFK—after a year and a half of breathless fiddling with Keynesian spending and the currency stratagems. And given that the easiest way to grow more was to get the income tax out of the way, Surrey's plan for an across-the-board rate cut would gain all priority—in the summer of 1962. But not yet.

In 1961, JFK did trot out something he called a "tax cut," a little bone for businesses. That spring, the Treasury prepared legislation providing for a credit against income taxes paid for companies that made investments in plant and equipment. The hope (as with Operation Twist) was that foreign dollars would be drawn away from gold redemptions and toward the stock of American companies, in that such companies would become more profitable on account of the tax credit.

The bill went nowhere, not least because JFK suggested over the summer that with the Berlin Wall going up in Germany, the government might have to think about raising taxes for defense spending purposes. (The defense tax did not come to pass.) In the meantime, opposition to the tax-credit idea emerged from business constituencies themselves. What the government thought qualified as tax-credit-eligible "investment" remained unclear and perhaps useless from a business perspective. Executives suggested that they had better ideas about how to lessen taxes on production, such as allowing more write-offs. As a Democratic congressman said as the tax-credit bill was dying, "A lot of us aren't going to feel any compulsion to vote for something which business keeps shouting it doesn't want."[9]

That was it. Treasury had spent—had wasted—all of 1961 juggling devices to keep the dollar good against gold. Thus did Dillon's and the Treasury's efforts over that first year complement those of the CEA and the government spending apparatus. Dillon tried artful tricks and fixes to shore up the dollar, while the executive authorities ramped up government spending. It was all of a manifestly short-term nature: moves to tide the economy over until a final economic policy could be identified and implemented that would break the recessionary cycle. The Kennedy culture in the first phase of the administration, as at least went economic policy, was to keep the problem at bay with artifice until the big administration plan was ready.

What was that to be? There was still a chance it would not be tax reform featuring a big cut in all rates of the income tax. The CEA, after all, kept throwing in for ever more government spending— "investment" in education, science, parks, and all the rest—while saying boo about a major permanent income tax cut. How alone was Stanley Surrey at Treasury?

All along in 1961, Dillon had his back. Dillon reiterated Kennedy's stated intention, of April of that year, that an across-the-board income tax cut would come in 1962. And he made it plain that he did not envision this tax cut as an antirecessionary move. It was to provide for sustained economic recovery as opposed to stimulus. "It is probable by this time next year our economy will be rolling into high gear. We may well be in the midst of an economic boom," Dillon said to a business audience in June 1961, speculating further that the boom he foresaw would lead to a rise in tax receipts, even a budget surplus. As the *Wall Street Journal* reported Dillon's statement, it added that Dillon "repeated earlier hints that a tax cut may be recommended by the Administration as a by-product of the business surge," and further that "the Secretary said it has not been decided whether this surplus will be used . . . for a tax refund. But he added that a tax reduction would probably be the course of events to expect."[10]

"Probably." Nineteen sixty-one thus came in like many a year in the Eisenhower era. Economic growth was 2.6 percent—the identical number as in 1960. The difference was that 1960 came on the heels of the whopping post-deep-recession growth of 1959, of 7 percent, and 1961 after a year with two negative quarters. If there was an argument for slack and potential unmet, it was materializing in the growth figures as JFK completed his first year in office. The unemployment rate stuck up over 6 percent for all of 1961, the first time that had happened over a calendar year since the data started being collected after World War II.

The stock market evinced good feelings. The Dow Jones Industrial Average churned up 15 percent through the spring of 1961, crossing 700 for the first time, as Kennedy enacted the Keynesianism and faked his way through the gold standard while still appearing to hold out the promise of a tax cut. The market dipped a little over the summer and fall, then surged right ahead through the last days of trading in 1961. When the markets closed for the year on December 29, the Dow was at 731, four points off its all-time high of two weeks before. This was an Eisenhower trend as well. In the 1950s, the market jumped with the little booms and plateaued with the busts. Corporate profits were always somewhat secure, despite the economic cycle, for all the tax benefits that could be taken advantage of.

Kennedy would cut tax rates, and big, within two years. It was actually there in the tea leaves of 1961. The secret was that he was not giving in on the dollar. The dollar would remain redeemable against gold at $35 per ounce under a JFK presidency, no matter what. Kennedy had done the Paul Samuelson/CEA spending, to be sure, over his first year, but these advisers had also insisted that their spending (and loose-money) plans would require an evolution out of the current monetary system. Kennedy remained completely unmoved on that score—completely.

This meant that the only way the dollar would remain tenable at its old storied price was that if demand for it surged and stayed high for the long term. The chicanery with the gold pool, Operation Twist, and so on would have to be dispensed with in favor of real policy. The only true marker of that was economic growth. If there was any further flagging on that score in 1962, the spending plans would have to be dumped for another alternative. And in would waltz Surrey's across-the-board tax cut, to "get the economy moving again."

Chapter 5

A TURNING POINT

Though Kennedy is today revered for his civil rights and foreign policy measures, his initial responses to integration activism and Soviet challenges alike were passive if not feckless. When in the spring of 1961 the Freedom Riders met mailed fists from segregationist radicals, Kennedy did essentially nothing, aside from asking for a "cooling-off period" so that the spectacle of domestic disturbances did not give the Soviet Union propaganda fodder. Similarly, his principal response to the Bay of Pigs defeat was to push it away, setting up commissions to study why it happened.

Fortunately, Kennedy learned from both disasters. Two years later, the next time a major civil rights crisis hit—in Martin Luther King Jr.'s Birmingham integration crusade—the president responded by introducing a powerful civil rights bill to Congress, the bill that became law as the historic Civil Rights Act of 1964. When a year and a half later, during the October 1962 Cuban Missile Crisis, Kennedy went up against Nikita Khrushchev, he got his adversary to back down and take the missiles out. Thereafter, Kennedy's reputation was not of a man who shrank from challenges (when not being bested by a banana republic dictator) but of one who called the shots against the biggest and most unsavory players on the world stage.

Kennedy's economic policy fit a similar pattern: initial misjudgment followed by a course correction. Big-time government spending and games to keep the dollar level against gold were the particulars of the Kennedy economic policy as enacted in 1961. The result was no break from the 1950s economic trends. Soon there would have to come another recession, and JFK would have to get policy right or be exposed as an attractive second-rater. Just as it was with Cuba and civil rights, his response was to gather the strength and wisdom to change course the next time the opportunity arose in all these areas. Kennedy would let the dangerous signals that came on the scene in 1962 shock him into a decisive policy shift.

The stock market did not keep up its December 1961 highs through the first months of 1962. By early April, the Dow industrials were off the December peak by about 35 points, or 5 percent, in a holding pattern. If the stock market was divining that something was a bit off in the spring of 1962, John F. Kennedy himself certainly supplied the dramatics. A little nonevent in the business world was about to happen, and from it there would come unedifying if colorful language and character assassination from the lips of the president. Over the thousand days of the Camelot era, the confrontation that Kennedy had with the executives of the steel industry in that month ranks at once as one of his worst and most unappealing episodes—but also as one that launched a turn from the CEA to Douglas Dillon.

The basic story was nothing much. In 1959, the national months-long steel strike had compelled the federal government to try to broker the next disagreement between labor and management before a work stoppage broke out. When Kennedy became president, he assigned his labor secretary, Arthur Goldberg, to be a liaison between the unions and the major steel companies so as to forestall the 1959 nightmare, when, as is now clear, the long strike began the era of American manufacturers' getting their steel from abroad. Goldberg met with the relevant parties religiously through 1961 and early 1962 and got it across that the president wanted labor peace—indeed that the president would seek to take punitive action against the side that he might perceive to be acting unfairly. On April 6, 1962, labor and management agreed to a new contract with hourly pay increases 40 percent below the union proposal.[1]

Kennedy was most pleased. Steel, "which bulks so large in the . . . economy that it can upset the applecart all by itself," as Heller had put it in a memo, would dedicate itself to production, sales, and employment for the remainder of Kennedy's term. Yet four days later, on

April 10, the president of U.S. Steel, Roger Blough, appeared at the White House and handed Kennedy a news release saying that the major steel companies were going to raise steel prices by 3.5 percent.[2]

Theoretically, that addendum should have been given during the negotiation process with labor, not after. Coming after the union representatives had agreed to the structure of wage increases meant that the proceeds of the price increase would flow entirely into management's and the corporations' pockets. It was against the spirit of negotiation since the 1959 debacle, presumably, for Blough and his side to have done such a thing. And as Kennedy feared, it might cause a run on the dollar, in that the dollar would buy less with steel more expensive.

Kennedy's response to the steel price increase showed a side of the man that had previously been rather unseen. Kennedy fulminated in anger. At his press conference the next day, reporters acknowledged to the president that they were taken aback by his "strong language." Take his opening statement:

> Simultaneous and identical actions of United States Steel and other leading steel corporations increasing steel prices by some $6 a ton constitute a wholly unjustifiable and irresponsible defiance of the public interest. In this serious hour in our Nation's history . . . when we are devoting our energies to economic recovery and stability, when we are asking reservists to leave their homes . . . to risk their lives—and four were killed in the last two days in Viet-Nam—and asking union members to hold down their wage requests at a time when restraint and sacrifice are being asked of every citizen, the American people will find it hard, as I do, to accept a situation in which a tiny handful of steel executives whose pursuit of private power and profit exceeds their sense of public responsibility can show such utter contempt for the interests of 185 million Americans.

Kennedy went on in this vein through the questions with reporters and then amped it up at home. The future *Washington Post* editor Benjamin Bradlee met the president regularly in his family quarters and transcribed in his diary these quotations of Kennedy's from that week: "It looks like such a double-cross. I think steel made a deal with Nixon, not to raise prices [until] after the election. Then came the recession, and they didn't want to raise prices. Then when we pulled out of the recession they said, 'Let Kennedy squeeze the unions first, before we raise prices.' So I squeezed [the unions]. And they kicked us right in the balls. . . . The question really is: are we supposed to sit there and take a cold, deliberate fucking. Is this the way the private enterprise system is really supposed to work? I can't go make a speech like I did [at the press conference] . . . and then sit on my ass. . . . They fucked us, and we've got to try to fuck them."[3]

And as the *New York Times* reported, in what became one of JFK's more immortal lines, Kennedy told his economic advisers, "My father always told me that all businessmen were sons of bitches, but I never believed it till now!"

Kennedy's practical response was to try to rescind defense contracts from the offending steel companies and begin an antitrust action against them. The FBI wasted no time in the latter matter, appearing at 4 a.m. before the doors of journalists who might have incriminating quotations from steel executives that bespoke collusion. Republicans called these "Gestapo tactics," and the major steel companies relented. Blough's U.S. Steel and its coconspirators rescinded the price increase three days after announcing it. The episode was over.[4]

A thought, however, began to arise across the nation: was Kennedy antibusiness? He was increasing government spending by 15 percent in two years and had proposed a corporate tax credit that executives felt was poorly formulated (though the investment credit was now reintroduced in the House with provisions more congenial to business leaders). He spoke often about how tax deductions were phony, "obtained by disguising personal expenses as business outlays"—Stanley Surrey stuff—without any palpable action on reduced rates. He essentially called the steel executives un-American and did call them and all their confreres "sons of bitches." Executives acted puckish that spring and began to stroll around with "SOB Club" buttons on their lapels. Businesses—and the economy as a whole— seemed to be turning against Kennedy.[5]

Then Kennedy reiterated an economic policy request he had made to Congress months earlier—a move called for by the CEA. On January 22, he had asked Congress to empower him, on his own discretion and on his own schedule, to shave income tax rates uniformly by a maximum of five percentage points for periods of six months at a time. He wanted to be able to reduce all the rates running from 20 to 91 percent to 15 to 86 percent, respectively, whenever he liked, and it would last for half a year. The point, as Kennedy put it as he signed off on his advisers' economic report for 1962, was that a "temporary reduction of individual income tax rates across the board can be a powerful safeguard against recession." In addition to the temporary tax cut authority, Kennedy also told Congress that he wanted summary power to extend unemployment benefits and accelerate federal building projects, also in the name of staving off recession—continuing along the lines of 1961. Kennedy was becoming oblivious to the fact that even in times of semicrisis, Congress does not make a habit of ceding plenary authorities to the president. What these hopeless moves showed was that by Kennedy's own more-than-tacit admission, recession remained a bias of the American economy two years into the 1960s.

Still, the CEA and Paul Samuelson were getting their wish, in that Kennedy was pushing ever more fully for their policy. The year before, in his antirecession task force report, Samuelson had publicly recommended a temporary tax cut as a "Second Line of Defense" to fight recession, should a year's worth of spending not prove equal to the task. Sure enough, 1961 had proved the spending a flop, so now it was the turn of the temporary tax cut. In the context of recommending this cut, Samuelson downgraded the idea of a big, permanent tax cut, on the grounds that such a full-fledged move might prove "tragic," given "the new public programs coming up in the years ahead."

Kennedy had not taken up this recommendation in 1961, possibly because he was cowed by the wide currency of economist Milton Friedman's "permanent income hypothesis," first advanced in 1957. Friedman's hypothesis held that people do not spend the money that comes from temporary tax breaks. Rather, they take into account the their long-term, lifetime income trend as they make spending decisions. This blunts the effect of any governmental attempt to "put money in people's pockets," as the Keynesian saying goes.

Now, however, times were getting ominous, and Kennedy thought the gamble was worthwhile. He told Congress, even more formally and explicitly than he had four months before, and even as he knew that Congress jealously guarded its fiscal policy prerogatives, that he wanted presidential authority to institute a five-point reduction on all rates of the income tax for six months at a time. Spending, tax cuts set to expire in the short term, fulminating at business executives—Kennedy's original paramount goal of "getting this country moving again," of more than doubling the rate of economic growth, was foundering in a morass of bureaucratic enhancement, policy trivia, and personal resentments in the spring of the second year of the administration.

At this point, the stock market started sagging, breaking out of the holding pattern of 5 percent off the 1961 high. By mid-May, the Dow was down 13 percent from the December peak. More down days came, and on May 28 the industrials fell by a hair under 35 points, a one-day drop in point terms not seen since 1929. The market struggled to come back, reaching a secular low we now recognize as occurring in late June, when the Dow bottomed to a level of 536, down 27 percent over six months.

Why the stock market was tanking was anyone's guess. It was fair to suppose that the market was judging JFK as disappointing. Defending the administration, Dillon said that the market had been overvalued (even though the Dow had first pushed through the 530s, indeed the 580s, in 1958). Just as well, it could have reflected collective exasperation on the part of investors at the administration's real economic policy. What was it—was it comprehensive tax cuts/reform and a good gold standard, or was it Keynesian spending and temporary tax tweaks and tricks in the dollar-gold market? Even as Kennedy had asked for the temporary tax cuts in January, he had added, just above his signature, these three sentences: "Later this year, I shall present to the Congress a major program of tax reform. This broad program will re-examine tax rates and the definition of the income tax base. It will be aimed at the simplification of our tax structure, the equal treatment of equally situated persons, and the strengthening of incentives for individual effort and for productive investment." If the president was going to implement this kind of reform advocated by the Treasury, when was it going to show up? Half following the CEA's plan and half following Treasury's was no way to inspire market confidence.

Perhaps recognizing the problems with half-measures, Kennedy huddled with his economic team and the decision that became the tax cut of 1964 took shape. Surrey and Dillon had been working for over a year now on the income tax cut proposal, stuck on the issue of balancing the rate cuts (the top rate going down 26 points, to 65 percent) with the commensurate amount of loophole-closing. Meanwhile, the congressional session that was supposed to be the occasion for the proposal entered its sixth month. Treasury's work was still not ready, but the essential elements were becoming matters of public discussion. The trade-off between rate cuts and loophole-closing was a thorny political issue. Any explicit reduction in or elimination of loopholes would raise the ire of favored constituencies, while the reduction in rates would reduce the value of all special preferences in the code.

Kennedy soon proved ready to endorse Treasury's product, on account of several episodes in what may well be called the president's "learning" at the hands of his economists. First, there can be no doubt that the CEA did win over Kennedy on one crucial point. Heller and others (including Samuelson) reiterated the argument that a budget deficit that results from well-conceived economic policy, namely one oriented toward economic growth, carries with it no material harm. Whether issuing from a tax cut or human-capital-related government spending, such a deficit will only presage growth in the private sector—a good thing. In a memo to Kennedy, Samuelson derided standard scaremongering over the "dread def—t." As events would unfold, the Kennedy tax cut would not in fact cause a deficit. Nonetheless, the elimination of fear that a tax cut *could* cause a deficit probably contributed to Kennedy's resolve to push through a tax cut.[6]

Kennedy's shift away from his CEA advisers and toward Treasury had been taking place for some time. Perhaps more decisive in Kennedy's thinking, in his education, as it were, in the late spring of 1962, was the interest that he took in a series of reports emanating from cosmopolitan sources. Both the Bank for International Settlements (BIS), of Basel, Switzerland, and the International Monetary Fund (IMF) issued white papers arguing that the United States should take a new approach to its fiscal/monetary policy mix. Instead of relying on Federal Reserve looseness to spark economic recovery, the monetary authorities in the United States should focus on one goal: price stability and the soundness of the dollar against other currencies and gold. In turn, fiscal—particularly tax—policy should take the lead in seeing the economy into recovery. "There is ample European experience to show that the possible internal restraint of a tighter monetary policy can be alleviated by fiscal and other policy means," averred the BIS report. This sentence was double underlined by Dillon in red in the copy he sent to Kennedy, "in response to your request this morning," June 8.[7]

The IMF report went on in a similar vein (Dillon also marked this up on JFK's request) about the necessity of using monetary policy for securing the dollar and the balance of payments among the United States and foreign countries, while relying on tax policy for domestic expansion. The IMF's conversion in this regard had begun the year before, when a twenty-nine-year-old staff economist by the name of Robert A. Mundell wrote a provocative paper. In November 1961, Mundell argued in an internal IMF memo that to get the United States out of the recession cycle, the nation should tighten money to solve the dollar-gold problem, and release fiscal policy to get economic growth. By 1962, the fiscal release had to take the form of tax cuts, because government spending had already failed to deliver economic growth. In 1999, Mundell would win the Nobel Prize in Economics, in part for his work outlining the case for tax cuts and a strong dollar in the early 1960s.[8]

While Kennedy was absorbing the BIS and IMF reports in June 1962, he went ahead and said that he was going to call for a permanent tax cut. On June 7, at his press conference, he made an announcement at the outset: "A comprehensive tax reform bill which in no way overlaps the pending tax credit and loophole-closing bill offered a year ago will be offered for action by the next Congress, making effective as of January 1 of next year an across-the-board reduction in personal and corporate income tax rates which will not be wholly offset by other reforms—in other words, a net tax reduction." Kennedy reminded the reporters that he was still asking for everything else—the temporary tax cut, the refurbished investment tax credit, the standby authority to spend on public works "in areas of heavy unemployment"—but this was the first time that he made clear that he was going to fulfill his promise of fourteen months before and present to Congress a major proposal for tax rate cuts. It would be a congressional session later than originally promised, but the measure would also be backdated to take effect at New Year's 1963.

Kennedy's staff was occupied at this time with preparing the commencement address at Yale University that the president was to deliver on June 11. Roger Blough (a Yale Law School graduate) was to be in attendance—as was indeed (and naturally to nobody's notice) an undergraduate named Arthur B. Laffer, whose 1974 diagram of how tax cuts can increase government receipts, the Laffer curve, would prove the most famous economics graph of the twentieth century.

The Yale commencement address was one of the more philosophical, and humorous, of Kennedy's presidency. It was the one in which JFK made the crack that Calhoun had quit the vice presidency because it was "too lowly a status for a Yale man." The main remarks, as Kennedy got beyond five introductory paragraphs of humor, sought "to particularly consider the myth and reality in our national economy." He referred, without naming them, to the steel and the stock exchange tumults of May and June, saying that the time had come for clarity and agreement on economic policy. "In recent months many have come to feel, as I do, that the dialog between the parties—between business and government, between the government and the public— is clogged by illusion and platitude and fails to reflect the true realities of contemporary American society." Kennedy's main example in this regard was the fiscal/monetary policy mix: "First, how can our budget and tax policies supply adequate revenues and preserve our balance of payments position without slowing up our economic growth? Two, how are we to set our interest rates and regulate the flow of money in ways which will stimulate the economy at home, without weakening the dollar abroad? Given the spectrum of our domestic and international responsibilities, what should be the mix between fiscal and monetary policy?"

Kennedy outlined the typical answers to these questions—budget deficits cause inflation, loose money causes a boom—and found them wanting. As an alternative, he brought up "the Bank for International Settlements in Basel, Switzerland, a conservative organization representing the central bankers of Europe, [which last week] suggested that the appropriate economic policy in the United States should be the very opposite; that we should follow a flexible budget policy, as in Europe, with deficits when the economy is down and a high monetary policy on interest rates, as in Europe, in order to control inflation and protect goals. Both may be right or wrong. It will depend on many different factors."

Kennedy did not, at Yale, explicitly call for a tax cut. He did not reiterate his pledge of four days earlier for an across-the-board cut in rates, of a "net tax cut," nor did he state (as he had in April 1961) that a rate cut would produce economic growth, courting the possibility of greater receipts from lower rates and increased foreign demand for the dollar over gold. He did suggest, however, that innovative macroeconomic thinking around the world was consistent with the idea of tax cuts and a strong dollar.

Kennedy came to the end of his speech with a mild swipe at the New Deal: "Some conversations I have heard in our own country sound like old records, long-playing, left over from the middle thirties. The debate of the thirties had its great significance and produced great results, but it took place in a different world with different needs and different tasks. It is our responsibility today to live in our own world, and to identify the needs and discharge the tasks of the 1960s." The political economy of the 1930s was unmistakable. There were large tax and spending increases and an epic devaluation of the dollar. If it was time to move away from those things "left over from the middle thirties," the direction had to be in favor of the tax-cut/strong-dollar policy mix.

Thus at Yale in June 1962, Kennedy identified, perhaps unconsciously, the general trend of Democratic Party political economy from over the course of a century and a half. There was a connection between

Calhoun's beliefs of the 1820s and 1830s and those that Kennedy was settling on, namely that the national prosperity requires a strong, reliable currency and a fiscal policy that encourages enterprise and makes no distinctions in doing so. The route of the 1930s—government intervention in the economy—was the exception to that trend. Expansionary fiscal policy could, however, mean more spending. Calhoun's great foil, the Whig Henry Clay, was a spender, on the American System internal improvements, whose professed purpose was to stimulate the economy. Calhoun detested this. He preferred comprehensive tax reductions, on the tariff, reductions that had the effect of lessening the value of the lines in the code that special interests had secured from congressmen. Kennedy had already tried the spending, and his CEA was calling for more. The tension had built: Kennedy had brought himself to the point where he had to make a clear decision about a marginal rate cut.

After the Yale address, calls of support for such a tax cut started pouring in. *BusinessWeek* took out space in the *New York Times* to print its editorial endorsing an across-the-board income tax cut, with the top rate reduced to 65 percent. Laffer curve arguments *avant la lettre* appeared: "Personal tax cuts should be made through reductions in each bracket. Because the excessively high top rates force the rich to seek sheltered investments, they are self-defeating. . . . Lower taxes mean higher taxable income, and this will enable the Treasury to recoup a good part of the lost revenue."[9]

The bombshell came on June 29. The Chamber of Commerce of the United States endorsed the same idea, a cut in all rates, with the top one cut to 65 percent, the bottom to 15 percent. Previously, the chamber had held out with the Republicans that no tax cut could come prior to reductions in spending. The chamber even said that it wanted this tax cut right away. If there were to be loophole reforms, they should come in a separate bill.

The chamber also followed up on the president's lead by saying that a major tax cut would alleviate the problems plaguing the monetary system. The chamber's chairman, H. Ladd Plumley, wrote in the statement calling for the tax cut, "Foreign bankers recognizing the energizing effects of this program will be less concerned about the stability of the dollar than they are at present." He added, "The program outlined is one, perhaps the only one, which will massively aid all the economy. . . . It will have double value—(1) It will be a needed immediate stimulant; (2) It will form a permanent tax basis upon which our economy could grow without recurrent recessions due to a faulty tax structure."[10]

The AFL-CIO, the labor union umbrella group, had already called for an income tax cut, conceding a big drop in the top rate so long as the lower rates were cut proportionately as well. Labor and management—they were in one embrace by early summer of 1962, even given the steel negotiation double cross of the previous April. The prospect of yet another recession, a fifth in thirteen years, was too much to bear.

Kennedy had some work to do. He had been as complicit as anybody in his administration in sending mixed signals about his economic policy preferences. He had spent 1961 and a good part of 1962 talking up and implementing the array of petty fixes to the recession and dollar problems, while referring to tax reform as if it were some event far in the future. Even at Yale, when Kennedy was clearly coming around to the Mundell/IMF/Basel view, his philosophical tone smacked of the noncommittal. Speaking of the two camps, the Europeans and the American balanced-budget advocates, who advocated opposite approaches to the fiscal/monetary policy mix, Kennedy said, "Both may be right or wrong. It will depend on many different factors." At a press conference in July, he responded to a question about whether he would be asking for a tax cut in 1962 by saying that "fine judgments have to be made."[11]

This was of a piece with how Kennedy had handled gathering crises to date. When the Bay of Pigs invasion failed in April 1961, he

groped for a Cuba policy that emerged only with the stunning events
of the missile crisis in October 1962. When the Freedom Rider out-
rages occurred in May 1961, Kennedy staved off big decisions on civil
rights for two years, waiting until June 1963 to submit the legislation
that would become the historic Civil Rights Act of 1964. In mid-1962,
there was a gathering economic crisis. Kennedy had manifestly dal-
lied in economic policy in 1961 and early 1962, no matter the assurances he had given to "get this country moving again" during the
campaign. The steel shock came in April, the stock market dive in
May, and after that a parade of business-executive visitors to the
White House who battered the president with their view that a recession was likely to arrive in the near future (forecasters were arriving
at the same conclusion). Circumstances called for final and definitive
policy—and Kennedy chose Treasury's recommendation: supply-side
economics.

Chapter 6

JFK THE TAX-CUTTER FINDS HIMSELF

Walter Heller made a strange comment to Kennedy about the Chamber of Commerce announcement. He said that a cabinet member had asked him, in jest, whether the CEA had drafted Plumley's statement in support of tax cut reform. His answer: "Good economics makes strange bedfellows." When it was clear that the CEA was actually disinclined toward tax-cut reform, why was Heller hinting that the CEA actually was on board with the chamber's statement?[1]

This marked the moment, in late June 1962, when the CEA began to realize that it was being superseded by Treasury in the president's economic policy, prompting CEA members to manage their rhetoric and public statements over the next two years such that credit for *whatever* policy the president adopted would fall to them. Heller's comment had the aspect of a prevarication, in that to date the CEA had had next to nothing to do with proposing, developing, or championing the kind of tax cut that Plumley was advocating on June 29. The idea of reducing all rates of the income tax by some 30 percent had been the Democratic ideal in Congress in the late 1950s, Stanley Surrey's pet cause in 1960, and the developing plan of the Treasury Department in 1961 and the first half of 1962. Indeed, the CEA had both dismissed the idea of such a major tax cut, in the form of faint praise and words of caution, and proposed an alternative long-term economic growth strategy focused on government spending. Moreover, the CEA had never endorsed the idea of strengthening the dollar through permanent tax cuts. Rather, the CEA and its ally Samuelson had pushed for loose interest rates and some sort of evolution out of the Bretton Woods system that would permit a dollar devaluation.

The only thing somewhat consistent with the chamber's recommendation for a tax cut and the CEA's own feelings on the matter had to do with timing and the nature of budget deficits. The CEA wanted a (temporary) tax cut right away, then and there that summer of 1962, and that was what the chamber now desired (permanently). Neither group was going to let the prospect of a budget deficit that might result from an immediate tax cut nix the idea.

But the magnitudes and durations under discussion were wildly different. Through July 1962, and in the wake of the chamber's announcement, the CEA kept pushing Kennedy for a temporary tax cut on the order of a two- to five-percentage-point cut in income tax rates. Plumley wanted a twenty-six-point drop in the top rate, and he wanted it immediately and for good. The package of advice with which the Ivy League Keynesians had been "educating" JFK for a year and a half was about to be studiously ignored.

As the tax cut that Kennedy chose in 1962 took shape and came to pass over the next two years, it was not the demand-side cut the CEA wanted. It was a marginal rate cut—the definition of a supply-side as opposed to a demand-side tax cut—and it erased the deficit because of an increase in tax receipts (and a diminishment of government-spending "stabilizers") that flowed from economic growth.

The summer of 1962 was also the moment when, in reality, the CEA ceded any primacy it may have had in economic policy formation—certainly that concerning taxation—to Douglas Dillon and the Treasury Department. Treasury had been working on a tax reform bill for a year and a half, and its hour had come. A problem was that the chamber wanted reform split in two: the loophole-closing staved off for a later date, and the rate cuts passed into law right away. Philosophically, Dillon was opposed, in that he did not want to lose the chance to close the loopholes. Practically, he knew that an immediate tax cut was impossible because the House Ways and Means Committee had signaled that it would not absorb new presidential tax legislation until Congress had completed work on the president's business tax cuts—a shrewd bill accelerating expense write-offs and providing a tax credit against capital investment that became law the following October. Dillon reasoned that it was better to prepare a complete bill, given that this was what the legislative schedule allowed. The only question was whether the economy could take it—it could tip into yet another recession if the wait for a rate cut continued.

Dillon therefore stressed to Kennedy that an absolute assurance of a major permanent income tax cut submitted to Congress by year's end eliminated all need for temporary tax cuts and emergency government spending, which is to say the CEA's continued proposals to keep the economy out of recession. As Dillon told the president (copying the memo to the CEA), "A temporary income tax reduction, . . . or a publicly avowed new or increased expenditure program, or a postponement of the postal rate increase, or agreement to a federal pay raise bill . . . would constitute danger signals of a loss of control, discipline or nerve that might have a counterproductive effect on confidence in the economy at home and the dollar abroad." The assurance of a marginal tax cut—made by both presidential oratory and avoiding further forays into Keynesianism—would be enough to hold the economy in modest expansion until the tax cut came.

Dillon further assured Kennedy that the Europeans were the ones giving the proper advice—supply-side advice. At a central bankers' meeting in Basel in July, Dillon told Kennedy:

> All believe that any significant adaptation of government policy aimed at stimulating economic expansion should be presented in a clear-cut, simple package [with] consensus on three points:
>
> 1. If there is to be a tax cut, it should be oriented toward improved business incentives; should be of a permanent and reform character; reductions centered on lower bracket personal incomes would be regarded as fiscally loose "bread and circuses," although some companion action in this sector would be understandable.

2. A deficit should be presented as the cost of essential tax reform. . . . Tight overall ceilings on expenditures should be announced. . . . It is also very important that deficits be financed out of current savings [as opposed to Federal Reserve looseness].

3. The Government should declare it is willing to allow interest rates to rise if combined demands from the private sector and a large Government deficit create upward rate pressures.

The consensus first proposed by Robert Mundell in the previous autumn, of controlled money and expansionary fiscal policy, then adopted by the Basel bankers and the International Monetary Fund, and that Kennedy found fascinating in the Yale address, was cementing into administration policy. The expansionary fiscal action would take the form of marginal tax cuts. On the monetary side, the Federal Reserve was about to do its part. The federal funds rate troughed in May 1962 and did not reach lows below 1961 levels again until the nation grappled with economic stagnation in the 2000s.[2]

In August, Kennedy began work on a speech explaining exactly what he wanted from Congress on income taxes, specifically why he felt large and marginal, if not quite immediate, tax reduction was the right idea. Still thriving on the chaos, he summoned for personal meetings all manner of interested parties and polled them for their opinions. A group of CEOs reiterated the consensus view in a statement read to the president in the Oval Office: "We continue, therefore, to recommend a change in the mix of monetary and fiscal policy as the best way of moving forward to correct a precarious position of the balance of payments . . . by permitting interest rates to rise. . . . The way to offset the effect of [this] action upon the lagging domestic economy lies in a reduction of taxes such as we have recommended," namely an across-the-board rate cut of substantial size. The businessmen dismissed the small, temporary tax cut proposal with jocularity,

referring to it as a "quickie," resurrecting the term used to mock one
of Senator Paul Douglas's Keynesian tax cuts in the 1950s, and "a nee-
dle in and then to be pulled out later on." At another meeting in Kennedy's presence, House Ways and Means Committee chairman Wilbur
Mills got Paul Samuelson to admit that he preferred temporary over
permanent tax cuts, leaving Samuelson frozen out of the congealing
Kennedy consensus.[3]

On the evening of August 13, Kennedy gave his speech, which was
broadcast on national television. This speech, along with another
along similar lines that Kennedy would give to a group of New York
industrialists and financiers the following December, clearly ranks
among the most economically sophisticated statements that any president has made on the impact of the tax code on the economy.

After beating around the bush for the first twenty minutes, Kennedy got to the core of his remarks: "Our tax rates, in short, are so
high as to weaken the very essence of the progress of a free society,
the incentive for additional return for additional effort." This line settled one disputed point. The administration's case for tax cuts would
not rest on the idea that they put more money in people's pockets.
Rather, the argument would flow from the fact that progressive taxation makes it less and less profitable to succeed. The more you make,
the higher your rate of taxation. This conferred great incentive effects
to tax rate cuts, which make doing well at work, be it as a laborer,
manager, professional, or entrepreneur, pay better after taxes (a point
Ronald Reagan would return to frequently in decades hence). Hang-
ing in the balance for Kennedy on this issue was "the very essence of
the progress of a free society."

Kennedy repeated his oft-made claim that "this administration in-
tends to cut taxes in order to build the fundamental strength of our
economy," but this time he added analysis and justification. He was
going to cut tax rates "to remove a serious barrier to long-term growth,
to increase incentives by routing out iniquities and complexities and

to prevent the even greater budget deficit that a lagging economy otherwise would surely produce. The worst deficit comes from a
recession . . . and this can be the most important step we could take to
prevent another recession. That is the right kind of tax cut both for
your family budget and the national budget resulting from a permanent basic reform and reduction in our rate structure, a creative tax
cut creating more jobs and income and eventually more revenue."

Kennedy was at pains to "emphasize, however, that I have not been
talking about a different kind of tax cut, a quick, temporary tax cut, to
prevent a new recession"—a slap at Paul Samuelson and the CEA and
contrary to his own suggestions of earlier in the year. Such an "emergency tax cut tonight, a cut which could not now be either justified or
enacted, would needlessly undermine confidence both at home and
abroad." Rather, Kennedy was announcing "an across-the-board, top-
to-bottom cut in both corporate and personal income taxes [with]
long-needed tax reform that logic and equity demand. And it will date
that cut in taxes to take effect as of the start of next year, January 1963."

Kennedy spelled out the logic: "Every dollar released from taxation that is spent or invested will help create a new job and a new salary. And these new jobs and new salaries can create other jobs and
other salaries and more customers and more growth for an expanding
American economy. . . . Our goal must be fuller [plant] capacity and
full employment and the budgetary surpluses that that kind of employment and capacity can produce."

And then Kennedy made the following arguments, suggestive of
the economics of Arthur Laffer of a dozen years hence, and of Robert
Mundell contemporaneously: "By removing tax roadblocks to new
jobs and new growth, the enactment of this measure next year will
eventually more than make up in new revenue all that it will initially
cost. By lightening tax burdens as the [European] Common Market
countries have done so successfully—and they have full employment
and an economic growth rate twice ours—it will improve the compet-

itive position of American business, encourage investment at home instead of abroad, and improve our balance of payments and will help make us all—individuals and as a nation—make the most of our economic resources." Tax rate cuts would raise the government's receipts and strengthen the dollar.

For some reason, Kennedy gave himself a grade of C-minus for the speech when the cameras went off. Perhaps he was regretful that he had spoken for so long before getting to his main message. This was a characteristic of Kennedy's speeches across all issues. His speechwriters (chiefly Sorensen) may have striven to capture the president's intellectual method as they did their work—going over all sorts of options and at last picking the most moderate one. Kennedy was asking for an across-the-board tax cut—a major move—but it would not be "quick," as he said, it would not happen right away, as certain constituencies and advisers wanted, though it would happen soon enough. Kennedy's tax cut decision was in this way moderate—and significant. It split the difference in the great tax cut policy debate of the late 1950s and early 1960s, with a bias toward marginality, permanence, and size.

Heller was crestfallen at Kennedy's speech. Dillon had, after all, prevailed over Heller (and Samuelson) with the president. As the speech was being prepared, Heller had handed Kennedy a list of six options that he could pursue—and Kennedy chose the sixth, the one offered by Dillon, an across-the-board income tax rate cut coupled with some reforms, to take effect early the next year. As Reeves wrote, "At the White House they joked that the President always agreed with Heller but always supported Dillon." After the speech, Heller gently admonished Kennedy to give yet another thought to the options preferred by the CEA. He wrote in a memo, "The most persistent question I have had about your tax-cut speech . . . is: Why did the President leave out a reaffirmation of his request for stand-by tax-cutting authority?" Kennedy had not, of course, so much left out the standby tax

cut idea from his speech as explicitly retired it as administration policy. "In some quarters, as you know, this omission is being interpreted
as backing away from the stand-by authority. . . . At your next press
conference, I hope you will find some way of once again underscoring
the importance of this measure and how timely it would have been if
we had it on the books now." JFK told Heller to "keep thinking" over
his ideas on tax policy and never breathed a word in favor of a standby
tax cut again.[4]

The task was now to get the whole economic team moving in the
same direction. Kennedy formed a cabinet council on economic
growth and put Heller in charge. There would be no more cogitating
on various economic-growth measures. There was going to be a big,
permanent marginal tax cut, and everybody had to come to agreement and speak in one voice in support of it.

In the meantime, in October, Congress passed Kennedy's business
tax cut. It enabled companies to subtract up to 7 percent of their own
investment in their enterprises from their yearly tax bill, and was coupled with guidelines to write off big equipment purchases against taxable income more quickly than before. The 7 percent credit perhaps
qualified as yet another loophole, one that business leaders had been
saying for a year they were tepid about.

The depreciation guidelines were something that American companies sorely wanted. Faster write-offs meant greater protection
against inflation. A write-off is a claim against taxation in the amount
of the deterioration of a company's production equipment. It does not
make sense, nor is it fair or economical, for the government to tax a
company's profits in their entirety if those profits come from sales of
products made by machines that wear out to some degree in the production process. The problem was that prior to Kennedy's action,
write-offs had to be spread over ten years, on average. If inflation went
way up, as Operation Twist and two years of Federal Reserve looseness implied it might, such write-offs would become valueless unless

they could be taken quickly. Kennedy sped up the write-off schedule. As the president said as he signed the October bill, his set of business tax cuts "provides a favorable context for the overall tax reform program I intend to propose to the next Congress."[5]

Also in October, Congress gave Kennedy the power he had asked for to negotiate tariff reductions on his own authority. This power would enable the United States to cut another tax barrier to economic activity, in its way similar to the income tax rate cut in the works. Clearly Kennedy was confident, as he took on his trade reduction authority, that his strong-dollar policy needed less and less artificial support. Free trade would lead to greater worldwide commerce in all currencies, including the dollar. Kennedy was displaying no fear that the dollar could now hold its own in this environment.

The business tax and tariff bills settled, the extended administration economic team took to working on the speech that Kennedy would deliver to the Economic Club of New York in December. This speech would serve as the last warm-up, the last announcement of the tax cut before it was introduced to Congress formally in January. Sorensen came up with a line and started chewing on it: "It is, in fact, a paradox—our potential budgetary surplus has not been realized because that surplus is too large."[6]

Kennedy's speech at the Economic Club of New York on December 14 had echoes of both the August television address and the Yale speech in June. At Yale, Kennedy had to encounter Robert Blough of U.S. Steel in the front row two months after the price increase flap; in New York, a phalanx of American businessmen—the "sons of bitches"—headed by David Rockefeller of Chase Manhattan Bank was in attendance. Kennedy arrived in his tuxedo, warmed up his audience with a crack about his Catholicism, and then buttered up Rockefeller. David was one of the namesakes of the Rockefeller Brothers Fund, which had sponsored the 1958 study that first put into prominence the idea that despite displaying some trappings of an affluent society, the United States was not growing enough, namely 5 percent per year.

"I know you share my conviction that, proud as we are of its progress, this nation's economy can and must do even better than it has done in the last five years," Kennedy began, after limiting his preliminaries to three minutes. The "most direct and significant kind of Federal action aiding economic growth is to make possible an increase in private consumption and investment demand—to cut the fetters which hold back private spending."

Increased spending, even of the private variety, the goosing of "demand"—was Kennedy turning Keynesian again? In one narrow way, he was. He conceded that cuts in rates of the income tax would cause a swell in day-to-day purchases, in that "consumers are still spending between 92 and 94 percent of their after-tax income, as they have every year since 1950" (a statistic he had gotten from Samuelson). However, a truly Keynesian tax cut would not have been marginal, as Kennedy's proposal was to be in its entirety. It would have been nonmarginal, an increase in deductions and so forth, with no cut in rates, much less all rates in a progressive ladder. (A Keynesian tax cut sees to it that individuals keep more of what they are already earning. A marginal tax cut enables individuals to keep a larger percentage not only of current earnings, but of greater earnings in the future.) As for the "demand" to which Kennedy was referring in the speech, it did not have to do with consumer spending, but specifically with "investment." Those with an eye to expanding current business operations or starting new ones—their "demand" for such things on "the supply side" (as a later generation would say) would go up with a tax cut.

Both of these enhancements, to consumer spending and to investment, would result from tax reduction, and only tax reduction of a certain sort: "The final and best means of strengthening demand among consumers and business is to reduce the burden on private income and the deterrents to private initiative which are imposed by our present tax system: . . . an across-the-board, top-to-bottom cut in personal and corporate income taxes to be enacted and become effective in 1963.

"I am not talking about a 'quickie' or a temporary tax cut," Kennedy went on with the old favorite turn of phrase, even though he had been an advocate of the quickie through the first five months of 1962. And he used the drug metaphor: "Nor am I talking about giving the economy a mere shot in the arm, to ease some temporary complaint. I am talking about the accumulated evidence of the last five years that our present tax system . . . exerts too heavy a drag on growth in peace time; that it siphons out of the private economy too large a share of personal and business purchasing power; that it reduces the financial incentives for personal effort, investment, and risk-taking."

Kennedy's case was that the government had gotten too big—this was why the private sector had failed to reach its potential and growth was hobbled. The solution lay in unleashing "incentives"—Kennedy used the word five times—for people to do better at business or while employed, on account of being able to keep more of their earnings. He used the term again: "To increase demand and lift the economy, the Federal Government's most useful role is not to rush into a program of excessive increases in public expenditures"—another slap at his own CEA—"but to expand the incentives and opportunities for private expenditures."

Kennedy said that he wanted the forthcoming tax bill to include "long-needed tax reforms," which is to say loophole-closing. This was "needed not only . . . to recover lost revenue and thus make possible a larger cut in present rates; they are also tied directly to our goal of greater growth." The present tax code "distorts economic judgments. . . . It makes certain types of less productive activity more profitable than other more valuable undertakings. . . . These various exclusions and concessions have been justified in part as a means of overcoming oppressively high rates in the upper brackets—and a sharp reduction in those rates . . . would properly make the new rates not only lower but also more widely acceptable."

JFK had rounded into form in his tax-cut oratory. Gone was the vacillation. There were no short-term and long-term tax policies at odds with each other, no weighing the potential of government spending to spark more growth than tax cuts could, no deep thinking on contrary options offered by his advisers and the international institutions. Kennedy was now determined that a big tax rate cut was to form the centerpiece of his presidency and that the economic growth that flowed from it would be his legacy, his accomplishment.

"I repeat," Kennedy continued, "our practical choice is not between a tax-cut deficit and a budgetary surplus. It is between two kinds of deficits: a chronic deficit of inertia, as the unwanted result of inadequate revenues and a restricted economy" (he had become familiar with this outcome in 1960 and 1961) "or a temporary deficit of transition, resulting from a tax cut designed to boost the economy, increase tax revenues, and achieve—and I believe this can be done—a budget surplus. The first type of deficit is a sign of waste and weakness; the second reflects an investment in the future."

Kennedy used the term that Sorensen had suggested to make the argument later captured by the Laffer curve: "In short, it is a paradoxical truth that tax rates are too high today and tax revenues too low, and the soundest way to raise revenues in the long run is to cut rates now. . . . The reason is that only full employment can balance the budget, and tax reduction can pave the way to that employment. The purpose of cutting taxes now is not to incur a budget deficit, but to achieve the more prosperous, expanding economy which can bring a budget surplus."

The businessmen and bankers at the Economic Club of New York had submitted their questions for the president beforehand. Kennedy gave answers to each of them after the nominated club member, Murray Shields, a New York investment consultant, read them aloud, press-conference style. The attendees asked if the Federal Reserve would print money to cover the budget deficit, and Kennedy reiterated what he had taken to referring to as his "Basel bankers'" point, saying no. In "the United States monetary policy is in some ways too loose, while our fiscal policy is too tight. . . . The international banks in Europe and others have suggested that the reverse would be more appropriate." They asked if he was secretly planning a national sales tax, and he dodged it (nothing of the sort was in the offing). They asked if the top rate was really going to go down to 65 percent, and he told them that they would find out in January, when Douglas Dillon would head to Capitol Hill with the administration's tax package. Kennedy had slayed his audience at the Economic Club of New York. Shields said, to close the event, "Mr. President, I ran out of questions. All I'd like to say is congratulations on your answers."[7]

Chapter 7

THE PUSH BEGINS

In January 1963, the Kennedy Treasury and the CEA at last spoke in one voice in support of a supply-side tax cut, namely a permanent reduction in every rate of the income tax, in the magnitude of about 30 percent for the top and bottom rates and a little less in between. Every January, the CEA is required by law to submit its *Economic Report of the President*. The CEA's effort in 1963 was, for the first time, an exercise in plugging a big, nonexpiring tax rate cut. The CEA had gotten the message: support the president's move toward the policy preferences of Dillon's Treasury. One CEA member, James Tobin, resigned, and made clear afterward with complete integrity that he did not prefer the administration's new policy stance.

There were some lines in this report that strove to save the CEA's face, to make it sound as if the whole idea behind the proposal was demand-side. These words, for example, were put in the portion of the report above JFK's signature, in the president's long accompanying letter of transmittal: "The most important single thing we can do to stimulate investment in today's economy is to raise consumption by major reduction of individual income tax rates." This was a bit of nonsense, in that reducing progressive income tax rates is specifically the kind of tax cut that gooses consumption the least. The report gave the game away in other lines: "Reduction of the top individual income tax rate from 91 to 65 percent is the central part of this balanced program."[1]

On January 23, 1963, Kennedy at last sent his income tax cut proposal to Congress. This document was prepared by Treasury, and its cover letter in JFK's name made the same points as the CEA report, shorn of the demand-side cheerleading. It announced that "the largest single barrier to full employment . . . and to a higher rate of economic growth is the unrealistically heavy drag of Federal income taxes on

private purchasing power, initiative, and incentive. . . . One recession
has followed another, with each period of recovery and expansion
fading out earlier than the last. . . . Our tax system . . . reduces the incentive for risk, investment, and effort—thereby aborting our recoveries and stifling our national growth rate."

There were three main elements to the tax-cut proposal that Kennedy sent to Congress. The first and the second of these were things
that virtually everybody was expecting, major cuts in income tax
rates, just as Surrey had outlined as early as 1959. Personal income tax
rates were to be cut by a maximum of 30 percent across the board. The
top rate of 91 percent was to go to 65 percent, the bottom rate of 20
percent to 14 percent, with each of the twenty-two tax rates in between
taken down on average about 22 percent. There was also to be a corporate income tax cut of a slightly smaller magnitude, of just under 10
percent. The top corporate tax rate was to be lessened from 52 to 47
percent, with slightly larger cuts for smaller companies.

The third element was also fully expected, the surprise residing in
the details: reform. The president's proposal would reduce or eliminate a set of some two dozen exemptions to income that otherwise
had to be reported for tax purposes. The most broadly applicable of
these changes to the population at large was a limitation on itemized
deductions—home mortgage interest, charitable contributions, and
the like. Under Kennedy's plan, such deductions would not count until they cleared 5 percent of taxable income; at present, there was no
such floor on itemized deductions. Another provision that would hit
tens of thousands of taxpayers was the scotching of the $50 exclusion
on stock dividend payments that had come with the 1954 tax bargain-
ing (a dig at Eisenhower). Still another was a provision to tax appreci-
ated property at death, before it came to heirs. Further proposals
included taxing certain life insurance and real estate arrangements as
well as sick pay, and the shifting of more income from the capital
gains classification (where rates maxed out at 25 percent) onto that of

personal rates. The provisions in the tax code that Kennedy was targeting for cancellation had been successfully lobbied for in recent years, and their enablers would surely fight to keep them—perhaps even fight to block the rate cuts so as to retain the full value of the exemptions.

Technically, it was only a detailed request, a recommendation, that Kennedy gave to the House of Representatives that day. Tax legislation must originate in the House, according to the Constitution. By the standard convention, Congress duly noted Kennedy's request, and the appropriate committee in the House, Ways and Means, convened to consider the request with an eye to writing a House resolution, a bill. The first step in this process was to hold hearings. The hearings began with the administration's representative, the secretary of the treasury, Douglas Dillon, submitting the tax plan along with all the supporting documentation—the research that went into it, on the administration's part. Dillon then made a statement and took questions from the twenty-five-member committee and returned for the same purpose several more times. In addition, all manner of public comment took place before the committee. Interested parties testified, by invitation from or application to the committee, on the president's proposal.

Getting the Ways and Means hearings off to a start on February 6, Dillon laid out the classical Stanley Surrey position: rates had to be cut, and as rate cuts devalued tax loopholes, a good number of them should in turn be retired. Dillon said to the committee, "The primary objective is to release the economy from the shackles of an overly repressive income tax rate structure so that it can . . . avoid the recurring recessions that have characterized the postwar years. . . . Removing the restraints imposed by our repressive tax rate structure . . . will restore incentives for risk taking, initiative, and extra effort—incentives that have been held in check in recent years."[2]

Dillon kept intoning the word "incentives" probably for a particular reason. He wanted to reclaim it. In recent years, tax loophole-mongers had co-opted the word. "Incentives" were not, in the tax parlance of the era of the 91 percent top rate, obtained by cutting tax rates, but by giving a favored constituency an exception from the high rates. As one of Surrey's legal colleagues, Geoffrey Lanning of Yale Law School, had said exasperatedly several years before, "It is argued that only a system of special preferences will provide the needed economic incentives." Dillon wanted incentives to be understood as flowing from lower rates, not exceptions from high rates.[3]

This trade-off did not go down well in the belly of the beast, the main congressional committee that had taken part in supervising a vast expansion of the tax code in the 1950s. Dillon began to get an earful that would continue unabated for the next six weeks. The defenders of the petty loopholes had effective allies in the Republicans in Congress, who made clear to Dillon that they opposed the tax cut for their same old reason: it did not wait for a spending cut to come first.

Kennedy had done himself no favors on this score in the State of the Union address of several weeks before, when along with announcing that he was about to send Congress the tax-cut proposal, he said he was also recommending more spending. It was a bad move. As events would play out, had JFK been a spending hawk as he introduced his tax-cut bill, he might have gotten it passed by Congress and signed into law by himself, before the assassination.

Kennedy had said at the State of the Union, "This country cannot afford to be materially rich and spiritually poor," nor could "the quantity of American goods outpace the quality of American life." Right then on January 14, as he was beginning his sales pitch of the tax cut to Congress and the nation, there he was pushing for more spending on such things as schools, job training, a domestic Peace Corps, a fledgling Medicare system, mass transit, and national parks. He had not shaken all of the CEA's enthusiasms. Yet a month before, in Treasury mode at the New York Economic Club, Kennedy had made clear, as he put forward his case for tax cuts, that "the federal government's most useful role is not to rush into a program of excessive increases in public expenditures."

"It's too bad President Kennedy didn't end his State of the Union speech about a third of the way through—when he was way ahead with his tax-cut proposals," a *Wall Street Journal* editorial put it the next day. "Instead, he apparently thought it necessary to tack on . . . a motley assortment of recommendations adding up to a 'domestic program.'" The *Journal* and the Ways and Means minority members were giving voice to the standard Republican reluctance to cut taxes in an era of big government, stock stuff since the postwar deficits became chronic in the early 1950s. Conservatives believed that taxes, especially at the highest marginal rates, had to be cut. They were loath, however, to concede tax reduction in the absence of demonstrated control of spending. If tax cuts were freestanding, the lever to ratchet spending downward would be lost. Moreover, conservatives wanted to give no berth to Keynesianism and the idea that deficits might stimulate the economy.[4]

"It's a waste of time to talk about lower taxes," the *Journal* editorial page had written in 1953, outside the context of cutting spending. Yet there was no recent record of this. Federal spending was projected to be over $100 billion in 1964, representing a two-and-a-half-fold increase in real terms since the postwar trough in spending of 1948. Even in view of the baby boom, this increase in federal spending over sixteen years was incredible. American population increased by a third from 1948 to 1964.

The Kennedy Treasury calculated that the rate cuts on the personal and corporate schedules proposed in January 1963 would result in $13 billion less in federal receipts, while the reforms would recoup about $3 billion, for a net loss of $10 billon, spread over the three-year phase in of all the provisions. However, as Kennedy himself said repeatedly, the increase in economic activity that the tax cut would engender (and owing as well to better capital allocation on account of the reforms) would lead to more governmental receipts. In the hearings, Dillon said that by 1967 federal receipts would be higher with the tax cut than they would have been without it. Surely this prediction was accurate. Federal receipts in 1967 were 17.8 percent of GDP, the highest mark since 1954. From 1952 to 1962, real federal receipts were essentially unchanged year over year; by 1967, they had leaped by a third.

Vermont Royster's page at the *Journal* looked askance at the proto–Laffer curve argument in early 1963, namely "the Administration's belief that its large-scale tax cuts would generate so much economic activity that its revenues would increase even with the lower rates. That is a possibility; it may even be a probability. But it is not a certainty. All that is now certain is higher spending and deficits." The *Journal* editorial page went on, "Tax-cutting is not at all the surest and soundest way to a balanced budget; that way is to reduce the spending. The Kennedy tax program may be fine by itself, but the Government's financial policy as a whole cannot honestly be called responsible. The saddest part is that there is every reason to believe that this nation's economy could really go places. It could, that is, if the President would only give the same serious attention to the spending side of the ledger that he is giving to the problems of our obsolete tax structure."[5]

In the hearings, Representative John W. Byrnes, Republican of Wisconsin, confirmed that he believed that tax rates were too high and had to be cut—"that our high and steeply progressive tax rates are a drag on our private enterprise economy." He said, however, that the administration's proposals in general, even prior to the present tax measure, always seemed to be aimed at the same broad things, "to cure unemployment, correct [the] balance of payments, give a better break to consumers, and everything down the line, and now we find this bill is going to do the same thing." Never in the two full years of the Kennedy agenda, as of early 1963, was there action on reducing spending. This was enough to keep Byrnes, and virtually all members of the Republican Party (save the few who were dedicated social liberals), from supporting the Kennedy tax plan.[6]

As Dillon strove to defend the tax cut in congressional committee, the coalition of the previous summer began to unravel. H. Ladd Plumley, the Chamber of Commerce chairman, found himself questioned by his own membership for calling for an immediate tax cut instead of holding out for spending restraint. The leadership of the AFL-CIO, meanwhile, indicated that it would prefer more extensive cuts in the bottom rate brackets, in exchange for trimming the rate cuts at the top. Kennedy himself kept up some demand-side rhetoric as he pushed the tax cut into Congress, though he continually said two things that qualified as supply-side. He wanted the top rates cut, even though the "propensity to consume" (the inverse of the propensity to save and invest) of the highest earners was small. And he insisted that lower rates on high earners would prompt such individuals to earn more. In his message to Congress, he summed up his demand-side and supply-side justifications in one sentence: his tax cut would "enable investors and producers to act this year on the basis of solid expectations of increased market demand and a higher rate of return."

As the hearings went on, the tone of the discussion went downhill. Representative Cecil R. King, Democrat of California, blasted those who had proved all too eager to testify. "I have a strong suspicion," King said in a statement as the hearings closed, "that some people appear at our hearings, or urge others to do so, . . . not necessarily to be constructive and helpful . . . but primarily to increase their retainers or income or make an impression on their associations." The pressure groups had been looking out for number one—themselves. King was outraged at the thought that "mere numbers of repetitious witnesses or the 'importance' of the witness alone should affect our decisions." Representative Byrnes, for whatever reason, called King's statement "asinine." Patience was wearing thin.[7]

As the hearings plodded along, and as each of the provisions, from the rate cuts to the esoteric reforms, became embattled, Kennedy himself introduced another justification for his tax cut: it could stave off recession. As he said at his press conference on February 14, a week into the hearings, "What I am most concerned about is the prospect of another recession."

Technically, this was another admission on Kennedy's part that the administration's first two years of economic policy had not been successful—that goals had gone unmet. The gamut of the recommendations of Paul Samuelson's antirecession task force (which is to say spending programs) had been put in place, most of them early, in 1961. But in 1963, here was Kennedy sounding the same notes as three years before, when he had gone on about "getting this country moving again." As he continued at the press conference, staccato-style, "In 1958, a recession, in 1960, a recession. . . . In my judgment, the best argument [is] that the reduction in taxes [is] an effort to release sufficient purchasing power and . . . to stimulate investment so that any downturn in business would be lessened in its impact and could be possibly postponed. Now, if we don't get have the tax cut, it substantially, in my opinion, increases the chance of recession. . . . So that's what it comes down to. And I think that . . . the tax cut should be looked at not as a method of making life easier . . . but with the desire to stimulate the economy and prevent a recession." Heller backed up the president, saying on television that the nation ran "a very great risk of recession" if Congress stalled on the tax cut. He added that any recession would be "far more costly" to the government than the tax cut, in that, as Kennedy had had said repeatedly in 1962, a budget deficit resulting from the former would be greater than that stemming from the latter.[8]

Kennedy started taking precautionary measures, should the tax cut not come to pass. The official reason for the February 14 press conference was to announce a new program, "to promote youth

On January 19, 1961, the day before he became president, JFK met with outgoing president Eisenhower to discuss ways to save America's sputtering economy. Also seated here *(left to right):* outgoing treasury secretary Robert B. Anderson, incoming treasury secretary C. Douglas Dillon, and Eisenhower's assistant Wilton Persons.

His economic ideas not yet fully formed, JFK addressed the nation's serious economic woes by calling for a strong dollar and more government spending in the 1961 State of the Union address.

Kennedy seemed to signal his belief in Keynesian economics when he appointed Walter Heller, shown here cradling his beloved *Economic Report of the President* in 1962, chairman of the Council of Economic Advisers.

JFK eleven days before the inaugural in January 1961, at the Cambridge, Massachusetts, home of Arthur Schlesinger Jr. *(right)*, where he received Harvard Law School professor Stanley Surrey's tax reform plan.

When Kennedy appointed Surrey, an advocate for major reduction of the top income tax rate, to be Dillon's tax assistant at Treasury, Keynesians were concerned, and Congress sat on the nomination for months.

JFK named Eisenhower's Undersecretary of State C. Douglas Dillon to be his treasury secretary. Dillon was a Republican and the son of a Wall Street broker as rich as JFK's own father.

Ted Sorensen *(right)* crafted JFK's tax cut speeches and introduced the "paradoxical truth" line, which Kennedy used to great effect as he justified his rate-reduction proposal to the Economic Club of New York in December 1962.

Robert A. Mundell, shown in the economics department of the University of Chicago, brought to light a developing global consensus when, as a junior staffer at the International Monetary Fund in 1961, he suggested that Kennedy should "reverse" his policy mix.

Arthur B. Laffer *(left)*, pictured here with Ronald Reagan, witnessed JFK's 1962 Yale commencement address, which suggested that Kennedy had been absorbing Mundell's points. Laffer would go on to introduce JFK's supply-side ideas to Reagan.

JFK met with his economic team in Palm Beach the day after Christmas 1962, a month before he would introduce his big tax-rate-cut bill to Congress. Seated on either side of Kennedy are the two persistent advocates of the rate cut, Dillon *(left)* and Surrey *(right)*.

After the House took three months to debate his tax-rate-cut proposal and still did not bring it to a committee vote in the spring of 1963, Kennedy began to suggest an alternative to the tax cut: more spending, even though that option had failed when he tried it in 1961.

The March on Washington for Jobs and Freedom of August 1963, capped off by Martin Luther King's "I Have a Dream" speech, mirrored the proposals aimed at economic growth and civil rights that Kennedy was trying to push through Congress.

In the summer and fall of 1963, southern Democrats in Congress implied that they would block everything, the tax cut included, unless Kennedy watered down or withdrew the civil rights bill he had put forth. But after Kennedy's assassination in November 1963, LBJ used his political acumen to ram his slain predecessor's tax cut through Congress.

Milton Friedman *(left)* gave Nixon the theory to take the nation off the gold standard. Once that happened in 1971, Nixon's best friend from the Eisenhower administration, Arthur Burns *(second from right),* now his Federal Reserve chairman, gunned the money supply like never before.

Paul Volcker *(right)* strove to cut down double-digit inflation from the moment he became the Federal Reserve chair in August 1979. Volcker and Reagan represented the monetary and fiscal arms of the supply-side policy mix pioneered by JFK and Dillon in the 1960s and, in the 1970s and 1980s, conveyed into policy discussions by Laffer, Mundell, and their allies.

In 1977, Representative Jack Kemp (R-NY, *left*) designed his 30 percent tax rate cut to "replicate" the JFK tax cut of thirteen years before. Reagan endorsed it on the radio that year and put it in his earliest policy statements as he prepared to run for president in 1979.

Jack Kemp and Larry Kudlow foresaw unfinished business in the twenty-first century: tax rates would rise, and the JFK-Reagan policy mix of tax rate cuts and sound money had to be applied once again.

BELOW: Office of Management and Budget chief David Stockman despaired of the tax cuts because deficits ensued in the 1980s. Reagan and OMB associate director Lawrence Kudlow (right) averred that growth would wipe them out. Within twenty years, the nation was so bereft of debt that Fed chairman Alan Greenspan warned there might not be enough remaining for the Fed to continue its open market operations.

To Larry Kudlow – With very best wishes & regards
Ronald Reagan

employment opportunities," in the president's words. Kennedy informed the press that 7.5 million students were expected to drop out of school in the 1960s, "entering the labor market unprepared for anything much other than unskilled labor, and there are fewer of these jobs all the time. . . . These figures reflect a serious national problem. Idle youth on our city streets create a host of problems." Federal spending would have to soak up these people, absent a real economic recovery. Commerce official William Batt indicated that in April the administration would probably have to increase public works spending, should the tax cut still be held up in Congress.

And held up it was. The hearings came to an end on March 27, when Ways and Means Chairman Mills put a stop to the public debate on Kennedy's tax proposal—without moving the bill ahead. The hearings had taken up an inordinate amount of time, occupying essentially the whole of February and March 1963, gobbling up twenty-seven days and producing testimony and documentation filling four thousand pages. At the end of it all, the proposal was, incredibly, nowhere near getting written up as a resolution and out of committee for a vote on the floor, an eventuality that would only happen half a year later, in September.

When April came, several aspects of Kennedy's tax plan were no longer. "Mr. Kennedy's proposal that itemized deductions be reduced by 5 percent of a taxpayer's income, the most far-reaching and hotly opposed reform in his program, is dead," reporter Robert Novak revealed from his poll of Ways and Means sources. Likewise, the repeal of the $50 dividend exclusion "is dead," and so on with a handful of other provisions, with the committee still giving consideration to stock option reform.[9]

April also brought news of economic growth. The cherished 5 percent level of annual growth in gross national product had been achieved in the first quarter of 1963, as it would be again in the second. "The economy's unexpected zip poses a special problem for President

Kennedy and his advisers," as one press story put it. "The President is trying to keep pressure on Congress by portraying a tax cut as insurance against recession in 1964." Facing facts, Kennedy made a pivot: he would bring back his original argument that a tax cut during a boom was just good policy. At this point in time, as he said to the press on April 19, "I don't see anything in the economy that would make the tax bill unnecessary. . . . It really wasn't very long ago when everyone was predicting a recession in the fall of '62 or the winter of '63. Now we have gone a longer period, we had a recession in '58 and '60, and we have been able to move ahead in 1963. . . . Therefore, I think it would be a mistake not to have the tax cut. . . . So I am strongly for the tax cut. And I think that . . . we are fortunate not to have had a turndown this winter or spring, which would have meant that the program we recommended"—the Paul Samuelson stuff—"was inadequate." Kennedy wanted to solve the problem, which had taken on the aspect of permanence. To do so, he had to smother the special interests, and the Republican naysayers, and get his tax-cut bill unstuck in congressional committee. He'd also have to take on an unexpected opponent of tax reform—southern segregationists.[10]

Chapter 8

THE CIVIL RIGHTS CONNECTION

Kennedy had won a substantial part of the African American vote in 1960, probably a shade over the 60 percent tallied by the Democrat Adlai Stevenson in the 1956 presidential election. Kennedy made this impressive showing among blacks even though as a member of Congress his credentials on civil rights had been nothing to speak of, and the running mate he had chosen, Lyndon Johnson, was possibly a segregationist southerner.

In the summer and fall of 1960, Robert Novak conducted a comprehensive survey of the attitudes and issue preferences of likely African American voters. He found that the economy trumped everything. "Despite the politicians' loud appeals for votes on the basis of civil rights," Novak wrote in late October as he presented his findings, "most Negroes are hardly listening. They're far more interested in bread-and-butter issues."

Novak published comments from hundreds of interviews he had conducted, all sounding a similar theme: "Kennedy is stronger on doing something about unemployment." "Because of the unemployment situation . . . I know the Democrats would do better for the working people." "When Republicans get in, everything flops." "We've got almost Hoover days now." And: "I don't know anything about civil rights. That's something that's going to go on for a long time." Novak predicted that Kennedy would capture an exceptionally large portion of the African American vote, and he did, perhaps 65 percent, that November.[1]

The swing of the black vote to Kennedy in 1960, as Novak had called it, reflected the mounting economic difficulties facing African Americans, given the repeated recessions, whatever major unfinished business there was in the area of civil rights proper. Among the most important issues confronting black Americans in the early 1960s was the difficulty of holding on to a job. The lack of good, consistent economic growth had created a scarcity of jobs that were both available and long lasting.

When Kennedy took office in 1961, black leaders welcomed his call for growth. In fact, at this point they saw the civil rights struggle and the mandate to revive economic growth as two sides of the same coin. "Without progress on civil rights," NAACP leader Roy Wilkins wrote Kennedy two weeks after the inaugural, "we shall be unable to achieve the full utilization of our manpower resources so indispensable to economic growth." Wilkins's view was supported by A. Philip Randolph, president of the Brotherhood of Sleeping Car Porters, a union whose membership was primarily African American. Randolph had come to the conclusion that without economic growth and opportunity, any progress on civil rights would be a dead letter: African Americans would not have enough money to take advantage of integrated lunch counters, transportation options, and stores.[2]

As the economic recovery came in tepid in 1961 and threats of recession emerged in 1962, Randolph revived an idea he had been entertaining for years. In March 1963, he decided he would hold a big rally in the nation's capital, the "March on Washington for Jobs." The march, according to its organizing documents, would "[draw attention] to the economic subordination of the Negro" while calling for the creation of "more jobs for all Americans." As the plans proceeded, 750 miles away in Birmingham, Alabama, the southern civil rights movement was reaching a fever pitch. Martin Luther King Jr. was thrown in jail (where he wrote his letter for the ages) on a bogus pretext, and safety commissioner Bull Connor's police dogs and water hoses savaged young activists and passersby, as appeared on television screens the world over. Randolph met with King after he got out of the lockup in May, and King decided to join the march. The title of the event would be modified to the "March on Washington for Jobs and Freedom." This represented a fusion of the two goals of the major activism regarding the plight of African Americans, namely enhancing economic opportunity (Randolph's main concern) and the closing down of segregation (King's). The march was to take place at the end of summer.[3]

The connection between tax reform and civil rights was not lost on defenders of the segregationist status quo in the South. Slow economic growth nationally, in particular in the North, was an important foundation of the segregationist cause. If frequent recessions disempowered African Americans, all the better. If frequent recessions meant that the brunt of layoffs and the increases in structural unemployment could be localized among African Americans and other minorities, northerners would become as fellow-traveling as southerners in the effective practice of racial discrimination. This would create a functional alliance between North and South on the need to go slow on civil rights. Progress on civil rights would mean that whites would have to start having their fair share of the bitter experience of unemployment. The lack of economic growth was part of the glue that kept segregation going. The initial destination Randolph had had in mind for the March on Washington—the headquarters of the AFL-CIO— illustrated this reality, so difficult to work with had the super-union proved to be as jobs remained scarce and Randolph pressed it to bring blacks in as full members. It was becoming apparent to civil rights activists that if good economic growth ever were sustained, people might stop caring about denying blacks jobs (given an abundance of jobs), and the segregationists would lose what national appeal they currently enjoyed.

The effects of slow growth and frequent recessions on the least fortunate in society came on full display in a book that became a sensation that spring and summer, Michael Harrington's *The Other America: Poverty in the United States,* which became a bestseller after the January publication in the *New Yorker* of a long and fawning review that Kennedy appears to have read. In *The Other America,* Harrington detailed how the constant recessions the nation was subject to created a vast underclass, and one not populated only by blacks. "In the fifties and early sixties, a society with an enormous technology and the ability to provide a standard of living for every citizen saw millions of people move back," Harrington wrote in the book's second chapter. "During this period the amount of unemployment considered 'normal' was consistently on the rise. After the 1949 recession, an unemployment rate of 3.1 percent existed inside prosperity; after the 1954 recession the figure had gone up to 4.3 percent; and after the business recovery from the downturn of 1958, 5.1 percent of the workforce was still idle. . . . In the matter of a decade, the 'normal' unemployment of 1958 was equal to the recession unemployment of 1949." Serial recession turned the "long-term unemployed" into "rejects, outcasts," while the economic growth that did occur became more concentrated in the ever-lessening majority not caught in the recessionary cycle. Harrington estimated that in New York City alone, in "a recession like that of 1958" and the "winter recession" of 1960–61, "their number is increased by a hundred thousand or so people who live on the verge of economic helplessness." Harrington wondered if not fifty million Americans, a quarter or more of the population, were trapped by poverty in the slow economic growth era of the 1950s and early 1960s.[4]

Harrington's preferred solution was to leave a good part of the challenge to renewed economic growth. He estimated that growth on the order of 5 percent could perhaps wipe out half the problem by the 1970s. Government programs were needed to solve the other half, he felt, the matter of the mass of rejects and outcasts accumulated in the substandard economy of the 1950s and early 1960s. Thus *The Other America* helped to usher in the welfare enhancements undertaken by Lyndon Johnson after Kennedy's death—Harrington did not foresee that the trillions spent on Great Society welfare after 1965 would itself have the pernicious effect of entrenching poverty.

Kennedy, however, had his own strategy, namely giving further scope to the first half of Harrington's plan. Kennedy would let economic growth carry the full load. The tax cut would prompt growth, returning the structurally unemployed to the workforce (and leading to declines in government's unemployment and welfare spending) while unlocking resistance to civil rights. By June 1963, Kennedy's legislative agenda reflected his aims in both areas. In that month, the president introduced a civil rights bill, such that the public accommodations King had been fighting for in Birmingham would be guaranteed in federal law. People started referring to the two pieces of legislation that Kennedy had before Congress that year, his tax cut and civil rights proposals, as his "big bills."

They were manifestly two sides of the same coin. From the tax cut would come growth, as the civil rights measure blessed the relaxing of racial discrimination that would flow naturally from that growth. Defenders of the racial status quo sensed this dynamic and proceeded with countermoves.

Senator Harry Byrd, Democrat of Virginia, took the opportunity of his seventy-sixth birthday party, on June 10, 1963, to indicate in a talk to the press that should the president introduce a civil rights bill (which JFK would do, nine days later), the tax cut might not even get the chance to be discussed, let alone voted on, in the Senate. Byrd said that a civil rights bill could bring a Senate filibuster. He pointed out that during a filibuster, senators are technically occupied, so committees cannot meet. In the event of a filibuster on civil rights, the Senate Finance Committee, the upper chamber's version of Ways and Means, and which Byrd chaired, would not be able discuss the tax cut bill should it get out of the House.[5]

It was clearly a threat, a sincere and powerful one. Indeed, two days after Kennedy's announcement that he would introduce a civil rights bill, 57 Democrats, mostly from the South, joined 152 Republicans to defeat, by 5 votes in the House, the latest Kennedy spending bill for unemployment relief and jobs programs. If Kennedy was going to try to do something about civil rights, southern Democrats would deny him his economic policy, clearly including his tax cut. It might be enough to get the president to renege on civil rights.[6]

Kennedy was now involved in political and policy stakes bigger than any he had previously experienced as president, at least in terms of his domestic agenda. These bills made his earlier Paul Samuelson laundry lists look small in comparison. This was not post office construction, labor surplus area programs, or early mailings of veterans' benefit checks meant to buoy the economy somehow, or a vanity project like the Peace Corps. The most ambitious Kennedy legislation to date concerned the space program. These new big bills really did promise to transform American life, along the lines that Martin Luther King Jr. had spelled out when he addressed the AFL-CIO in 1961, and as he would famously reprise in his keynote speech at the March on Washington. As King said in 1961, he harbored a "dream of equality of opportunity, of privilege and property widely distributed . . . the dream of a country where every man will respect the dignity and worth of human personality—that is the dream."[7]

Generally, the civil rights leaders were men and women of the left, interested, as economic policy went, in old-fashioned means of extracting more money from the upper classes. Randolph's policy focus for decades had been on such things as raising the minimum wage and ensuring full African American membership in unions that could collectively bargain for higher wages and benefits. Kennedy's argument for his policy, in particular his growth-oriented tax rate cut by which the economic pie would get much bigger, introduced a new and innovative consonance with the economic views of the leftist civil rights leaders. Kennedy's argument was that confrontation would become unnecessary, that economic growth would enable civil rights aspirations on all fronts to be easily realized.

Kennedy was a cool character, and he had handled Khrushchev with amazing sangfroid during the missile crisis the year before, but as his big bills came on the scene together in the summer of 1963, he got a little disoriented and lost some of his characteristic effectiveness. He started hammering away at the recession theme again, with a note of exasperation and uncontrollability. At a speech in California on June 8, several days before he announced the civil rights bill, he was heckled by a crowd holding up signs that read FREEDOM IN ALABAMA and HUMAN RIGHTS ARE NOT DEBATABLE. At his speech before a women's breakfast, he used the word "recession" ten times in three minutes.[8]

He went on in this way, almost unable to stop himself: "We have proposed a [tax] reduction this year . . . on the assumption . . . that the taxes which were passed during the Second World War and in Korea put such a drain on our economy that . . . the burden of that taxation strangled the recovery and we moved from recession to recession with higher and higher rates of unemployment." He continued:

> I think we have a chance. I know all the arguments against it, because I have heard them over and over again. . . . But we are going to have this program, I can assure you, or we are going to move into a recession, as we did in the 1950s when we moved through three of them. And we cannot afford to move from recession to recession with an unemployment rate of 5.7, .8, and 6 percent, and then move into another recession and come out of that recession with an unemployment rate of 7 percent, and then move along and stagger along for 24 months and move into another recession and come out of that with an unemployment rate of 8 or 9 percent.
>
> We are going to have coming into the labor market a year from now one million more young boys and girls. . . . So we are faced with very complicated problems which require complicated solutions. It is not as easy as it was in the 1930s, in a sense, to talk about minimum wage and social security—the old slogans.

And then truly scattershot stuff, with shades possibly of Harrington:

> We had a federal civil service exam, the basic exam, for getting a job in the government taken in the South recently. Fourteen hundred Negroes applied; 80 passed—80 passed! It is not their fault, but how can they pass if 40 percent of them have had less than 5 years in school? And they vote. They are citizens. . . . So there is a lot of unfinished business. . . . Will you tell me why this rich country of ours should have 3 percent of our children mentally retarded while Sweden has 1 percent? The reason, of course, is that they grow up in slums, that the mothers do not have prenatal care, they do not have special teachers—all of the things that will make it possible for us. We have set up the largest program in this country which has passed the Senate, and will pass the House, to make it possible for us to cut our statistics down from 3 percent who are mentally retarded, I hope down to a figure which they have reached already in some sections of Western Europe.

In the latter months of 1962, Kennedy had come into his own as a master of tax-cut and economic policy oratory. He spoke resonant lines of how "our tax rates, in short, are so high as to weaken the very essence of the progress of a free society, the incentive for additional return for additional effort," and of the "paradoxical truth" of lower rates and higher receipts, and of how "the purpose of cutting taxes now is . . . to achieve the more prosperous, expanding economy which can bring a budget surplus." But all that had come before Kennedy had a real bill pending in Congress, let alone real adversaries lining up against his whole agenda should he push for civil rights. As the pressure mounted in the summer of 1963, Kennedy's words on tax cuts and economic policy became worried and rushed and suggested a note of panic. The push to see the tax-cut bill into law would require a recovery of the faculties on the president's part that had brought it so far to date.

As the summer of 1963 waned, Kennedy was under personal as well as political pressure. Not only was he bearing weighty responsibility for the future of the country, but he was also mourning the death of his son Patrick, who died on August 9 after living for only two days. But even as he grieved, he kept up the push for the two big bills.

To Kennedy's relief, Wilbur Mills got a tax-cut resolution written up in Ways and Means that stood to please enough members on that panel and in the House at large. The administration helped him by caving in on previously key issues. The top rate would be taken down only to 70 percent, not 65. Given that the current top rate was a phantom rate anyway, applicable to next to nobody, even the very highest earners, it was not much of a compromise.

The way the committee accounted it, the reforms were reduced by a factor of more than three-fourths. The original loophole-closing proposed by the administration would have netted the government $3.4 billion in tax receipts. The new number was $800 million. Part of that $800 million in revenue retainment was explicitly the result of a rate cut. The decision on the stock option matter was to make the whole gain taxable at a new, reduced long-term capital gains rate of 21 percent, down from 25. The committee made a Laffer curve argument that this counted as a reform, as a loophole-closing, because it would increase receipts. As the *Congressional Quarterly Weekly Report* put it, the revenue effect would be a "$340 million gain" to the government, "due largely to expected heavy selling of securities by individuals who want to benefit from lower rates."[9]

The March on Washington for Jobs and Freedom occurred on August 28 and was a tremendous success. In his speech at the event, Randolph said that "it falls to us to demand new forms of social planning to create full employment"—a standard line of the left, but shorn of "planning" quite similar to what Kennedy had been saying about his own tax-rate-cut economic program. Randolph implied that he knew this, as he further said on the steps of the Lincoln Memorial that day, "We have no future in a society in which six million black and white people are unemployed and millions more live in poverty."[10]

King capped off the march with his now-revered "I Have a Dream" speech. Kennedy watched on television from the White House and had King, Randolph, and several other of the event's leaders over to decompress afterward. Randolph told Kennedy that the civil rights bill had no hope for passage unless the cause became a "crusade," and "nobody can lead that crusade but you."[11]

The crusade seemed to be working. Five days later, on Labor Day, George Meany, the AFL-CIO leader, said that "joblessness aggravates race discrimination and race discrimination weakens the economy," adding that "until the nation can solve unemployment, it cannot deal effectively with the struggle for civil rights and equal job opportunity." As historian William P. Jones has observed, Meany even went so far as to suggest that "federal authorities should prioritize tax cuts aimed at expanding the economy over civil rights laws that would ensure equal access to jobs and services."[12]

On September 10, the Ways and Means Committee approved the reformulated tax-cut resolution, all Democrats for and Republicans against, thereby introducing it for discussion and a vote in the House of Representatives as a whole. Republicans (led by Representative Byrnes) made an unsuccessful effort to link the 1965 installment of the tax cut to the government's keeping to a spending and debt ceiling. Mills countered with more Laffer curve arguments, inserting a statement in the resolution holding "that tax revenue produced by the stimulation of the economy through tax cuts first be used to eliminate budget deficits and then to reduce the national debt."[13]

Getting the bill out of committee was an achievement, to be sure. But the real hurdles lay elsewhere. The bill had to be scheduled for floor debate and a vote, and the head of the House Rules Committee, Representative Howard W. Smith, Democrat of Virginia, was a committed racial segregationist. Smith let it be known that he was working with Republicans to spike the bill with amendments so that it would become unpalatable to the majority. Mills planned to warn Smith that Ways and Means could take other parliamentary action to ensure that the bill as it emerged from committee could be put to a full floor vote.[14]

The bill was scheduled for initial floor discussion in the full House of Representatives for the morning of Monday, September 16. Some twenty-four hours prior to that time, on the morning of Sunday the fifteenth, the most horrific outrage in the long civil rights movement, at least since the monstrous murder of Emmett Till eight years to the day before the March on Washington, occurred. An explosion tore through the 16th Street Baptist Church in Birmingham, killing four girls, aged eleven to fourteen, as they were about to settle into their seats. The luminous atmosphere that had hung over the nation after the March on Washington and the "I Have a Dream" speech was broken. White supremacists had planted dynamite at the church; the first of them would go to trial fourteen years later, in 1977.

It was happenstance that the first scheduled order of business for Congress the next time the gavel fell after this event was the discussion of the tax cut. But the church bombing altered the tax bill's legislative fate considerably. It put the southern Democratic segregationists on their heels. It was not possible in the immediate aftermath of the killings to make a show of opposition to the tax cut so as to get a compromise on civil rights. Indeed, after September 15, the strategy that such southern Democrats pursued was to encourage the liberals of both parties incensed at the church bombing to strengthen the civil rights bill, on the chance that this might make that bill unpassable in one or both houses of Congress.

In the ten days that followed Birmingham, the tax bill's fate was

sewn up in the House. The first move came in the form of a remarkable introductory statement by Wilbur Mills, a statement probably
written by Norman Ture, the Stanley Surrey understudy who would
reappear in the Reagan Treasury in the 1980s. "As author of Section 1
[concerning the tax-rate cuts] of the bill," the Mills statement began, "I
would like to explain its intent and purpose. The purpose of this tax
reduction and revision bill is to loosen the constraints which present
federal taxation imposes on the economy." Mills offered that there
were two "roads" that economic policy could take, those of government spending and tax reduction. Both might lead to a larger
economy—but only the latter course would achieve the result through
private-sector expansion. "When we, as a nation, choose this road, we
are at the same time rejecting the other road, and we want it understood that we do not intend to try to go along both roads at the same
time." Mills then asserted his confidence that this tax cut would raise
government receipts. In view of this, he demanded that spending vigilance be maintained: "We are confident that within a relatively short
period of time, tax reduction and revision will result in larger federal
revenues than those we could expect without these tax changes. Section 1 of the bill calls upon both the Executive and the Congress to
restrain Government expenditures so that this increase in revenues
can reduce deficits and bring us sooner to realization of the goal of a
balanced budget in a prosperous economy."[15]

Following this thundering beginning, there was efficient debate
and then a vote on the unamended version that had come from Ways
and Means. Representative Byrnes tried to attach a rider requiring
yearly federal spending to be kept under $100 billion for the tax cut to
remain in force. All but one Republican in the House voted for the
amendment, joined by 27 Democrats, mainly southerners, and it lost,
short 14 votes. The Ways and Means resolution then passed the House
on September 25 by a vote of 271 to 155. The John F. Kennedy tax cut
was on its way to the Senate.

The bill passed the House with nearly nine of ten Democrats voting in favor (223 were for, 29 opposed) and more than seven of ten Republicans voting against (48 for, 126 opposed). Democratic supporters included Representatives Tip O'Neill of Massachusetts (who would be Speaker of the House during the Reagan years), Dan Rostenkowski of Illinois (who would be chair of Ways and Means), and Randolph's associate Adam Clayton Powell of New York. Republican supporters were nearly all eastern liberals, such as Representatives James Auchincloss of New Jersey (the cousin of Jacqueline Kennedy's stepfather) and John V. Lindsay (of Manhattan's silk-stocking district) and Charles Goodell (father of the football commissioner), both New Yorkers. New York Republican governor Nelson Rockefeller also was in favor of a major cut in tax rates along with a rise in interest rates—the Kennedy policy mix—on the condition that spending be clamped down, a position that observers found puzzling on account of New York State's runaway spending and taxes masquerading as "fees."[16]

Aside from southern Democrats who voted against, Republican nays included Representative Donald Rumsfeld of Illinois, who eleven years later would be chief of staff to President Gerald R. Ford, himself in September 1963 a representative from Michigan who voted against. Another Republican negative came from Representative Robert Taft Jr., despite his father's success in having brought a tax cut in 1948. The only member to vote "present" was Representative William Fitts Ryan of New York. He was pouting because he had tried to introduce loopholes into Kennedy's tax-cut bill and had been laughed off.

Byrnes had gone on television the previous week to inform the nation why the Republicans were opposed to the tax cut. "Our disagreement is not so much with what the president did say as with what he did not say," Byrnes said, referring to Kennedy's own speech on the tax cut on its introduction to the full House. "Desirable as it is to cut rates, we cannot talk about it responsibly unless we first discover the close relationship between taxes, spending, and debt. This the president did not do." Byrnes went on to point out that in 1948, spending was plummeting on account of demilitarization, and that was why Republicans pushed for a tax cut then, "in spite of three vetoes by a Democratic president [Truman]." He found it "interesting to note here that President Kennedy was against the 1948 tax cut when he was a member of the House." Perhaps, Byrnes implied, Kennedy's real desire lay in deficit spending. Mills had insisted in his September 16 message that revenue gains from the tax cut had to be used to cut down the deficit rather than to fund new spending. Whether JFK would have been vigilant on this score is something we shall never know, on account of the assassination in November.[17]

As for Truman himself, seventy-nine years of age at this point, earlier in September he had expressed disapproval of the tax cut, saying that the budget should be put in balance first. Kennedy responded to his Democratic predecessor's statement with an audible chortle on NBC television, calling on lines that had become practiced and finding his old oratorical élan:

> The reason the government is in deficit is because you have more than four million people unemployed, and because the last five years you have had rather a sluggish growth, much slower than any other Western country. I am in favor of a tax cut because I am concerned that if we don't get the tax cut that we are going to have an increase in unemployment and that we may move into a period of economic downturn. We had a recession in '58, a recession in 1960. We have done pretty well since then, but we still have over four million unemployed. I think this tax cut can give the stimulus to our economy over the next two or three years. I think it will provide for greater national wealth. I think it will reduce unemployment. I think it will strengthen our gold position. So I think that the proposal we made is responsible and in the best interests of the country. . . . I think our whole experience in the late

'50s shows us how necessary and desirable it is. My guess
is that if we can get the tax cut, with the stimulus it will
give to the economy, that we will get our budget in balance quicker than we will if we don't have it.[18]

As the tax cut got shipped off to the Senate, it was now supported
fulsomely within the administration by the CEA as well as Treasury,
and it was scheduled right away for hearings in Byrd's Finance Committee. In the wake of Birmingham, the House was busy marking up
a bigger civil rights bill, so there was no filibuster to clog up the Senate, at least not yet. Byrd would apply, or at least countenance, another
tactic to stall the tax cut. He would let the Finance hearings go on in-
terminably. This was shades of what had happened in Ways and
Means, but only superficially. What had hung up the bill in the House
committee was special-interest pleading that loopholes not be closed.
With most of those loopholes gone, the Finance Committee's slowness
was pure foot-dragging.

Hearings opened in October, and Dillon offered more capitula-
tions to get the bill through. He scratched the idea of a lower capital
gains rate, the thing that the House had just inserted to raise revenue.
It did not matter. Byrd and Democratic senator Albert Gore Sr. of Ten-
nessee were bent on having the hearings go on, waiting to see the degree of support for the civil rights bill. Gore had already informed the
administration that he was implacably opposed to the tax cut. The
year before, he had written the president, "The graduated income tax
is a hallmark of a democratic society and, at the same time, is one of
the most important mechanisms for the preservation of economic
democracy. . . . That a Democratic administration would attack the
graduated income tax by proposing a drastic lowering of the top
brackets and only minor reductions in the lower brackets, thus making the graduations much less steep, is untenable."[19]

This was a misrepresentation of the tax cut. On a percentage basis, the top and middle-rate brackets were being cut by the same amount. The top rate was to go down from 91 to 70 percent, a 23 percent drop, a similar percentage for most of the rates below that. The very bottom rate of 20 percent got the biggest cut of all, a full 30 percent, with that rate going down six points to 14 percent. Gore's statement further reflected a degree of perhaps willful ignorance of the facts about the tax code that had been laid bare in Congress over the last several years—namely that the top rates were largely inoperative phantom rates anyway, on account of all the exceptions.

It is possible that Gore and other southern Democratic opponents of the civil rights bill realized that there was an advantage to a steeply progressive tax code that served to slow down economic growth across the country. As A. Philip Randolph had come to know, northern labor unions were interested in practicing racial segregation and exclusion when the economy was in a fragile state. The power to discriminate was valuable in times of economic distress and uncertainty—and less valuable in good times. Gore may well have feared that the lessening of tax progressivity in the context of a major tax rate cut would prove so beneficial to the economy nationally that labor unions might become bereft of a good reason to maintain their fellow-traveling with southern segregationists. A slow economy delivered northern allies to Gore in the fight against racial progress. Opposition to the tax cut was therefore not inconsistent with Gore's interest in perpetuating the racial status quo. In the hearings, Gore confirmed to Dillon that he had been pleading with Kennedy to fire him since his appointment to Treasury in 1961.[20]

Gore lingered on so many questions in the hearings, with nary an objection from Chairman Byrd, that "Gore's tactic clearly amounts to a small filibuster," as one press analysis put it. The Democratic National Committee tried to get local politicians to oppose Gore, saying in a mailing to local party leaders that "he was making a most serious mistake" in his anti-tax-cut activities. The *New York Times* sized things up this way: "Many seemed to admire Mr. Gore's political audacity in defying the Kennedy Administration and the Democratic party on the issue." On November 14, Kennedy called on the Senate Finance Committee to get its work over with. He said the tax-cut hearings had already been "quite voluminous." As for the climb that the civil rights bill faced in Congress, Kennedy conceded that "the tax bill may be caught up in that. I suppose that some people are hopeful that that is so, but I am not." The next day, Byrd quashed a motion to end debate, ensuring that the bill would not get out of the Senate that year.[21]

As was unimaginable at the time, these would turn out to be the very last days of John F. Kennedy's life. Almost as if JFK had a premonition that his time on earth would not be long, he was palpably striving to make the most of every moment, as many observers noted. On trips that November, he said things to his associates such as "I have a feeling it's going to be a great day" and "I love this job, I *love* every second of it."[22]

Even as he reached his acme, Kennedy made a major mistake in his last month—supporting the assassination of President Ngo Dinh Diem of South Vietnam on November 2, an action from which that nation would never recover and that paved the way for the tens of thousands of American dead to come there. But on the domestic policy side, JFK had rounded into form. As he told the AFL-CIO on November 15, speaking of his big bills, the civil rights bill was crucial, but his tax cut was essential, in that "no one gains from a full-employment program if there is no employment to be had; no one gains by being admitted to a lunch counter if he has no money to spend; no one gains from attending a better school if he doesn't have a job after graduation." It is hard to envision that had Kennedy lived, he would not have bested his remaining tax-cut opponents, as well as the segregationists who disguised their aims as progressivism.

Chapter 9

BILL'S PASSAGE

Seven days after his tax reform bill was held back, on Friday, November 22, Kennedy was killed in Dallas. In the speech planned for Austin later that day, Kennedy's script had it that "we need a tax cut . . . as an assurance of future growth and insurance against an early recession." But JFK was gone now, and the presidency, the government, and the nation were thrown into a state of shock and disorientation before settling into a time of mourning.

The new president, Lyndon Johnson, had spent the weeks before the assassination wondering about his status within the Kennedy administration. He had been receiving strong signals that JFK would dump him on his reelection ticket in 1964 (possibly in favor of his brother Robert F. Kennedy), only to be assured that the very visit to Johnson's home state of Texas on November 21–22 indicated that JFK had made the decision to stick with his vice president. It is conceivable (if it could be imagined) that had Kennedy been assassinated several days earlier, and not in Texas—where the assassination would in macabre fashion cement the idea that JFK and LBJ were a team—Johnson as president would not have felt particularly beholden to the Kennedy agenda.

But Kennedy was killed making a visit to Texas, Johnson's home turf. Possibly the last words spoken to him were by the governor's wife, who told him in the limousine convertible, "You can't say Dallas doesn't love you, Mr. President." All of Texas loved Kennedy, and LBJ would stand with his state. After Johnson grimly took the oath of office on the plane back to Washington, he was determined to prove a loyalist to his slain superior.

The first matter Johnson had to contend with was the tendered resignations of Kennedy's staff. Refusing to accept their resignations, he kept the whole Kennedy economic policy team on board, Dillon and

Heller included. On the outs as he had been from the inner circle of the Kennedy policy deliberations, Johnson asked the economic team if Kennedy had really wanted the tax cut, and would they recommend pushing forward. They affirmed Kennedy's strong desire for the tax cut, and LBJ made it his top priority as the new president.

Fortuitously, the specific challenge that the tax cut faced at this time was the area of Johnson's expertise: getting it through congressional posturing and into law. Johnson, who had been the "Master of the Senate," as Robert Caro called him, relished more than anything else the challenge of getting a contested bill through Congress. Knowing where the sticking points in the bill would be, he turned his attention to doing the wheeling and dealing necessary to keep the tax cuts moving forward.

Along with enjoying the fight, it is also probably the case that Johnson fancied the opportunity to succeed where Kennedy might have been failing. Kennedy had gotten the tax-cut bill out of the House, but not the Senate. As all JFK's rhetoric had indicated, this was supposed to be his administration's signature bill, its main domestic achievement. Here it was still not passed after the thousand and some days cut off by the assassination. The civil rights bill was an even more slow-moving story. Kennedy had not even offered it until five months before the assassination. One thing is clear: other than the two big bills on taxes and civil rights that Kennedy submitted in 1963, his administration's third year, the presidency that ended on November 22 would have had nothing truly major in terms of domestic legislation to show for it.

Johnson realized the advantage of getting the tax-cut bill through the Senate right away, as a memorial to Kennedy. If he did so quickly enough, it would show one way in which LBJ was superior to JFK: he could move things along. In the face of LBJ's pressure (and the pain of the assassination), resistance against the tax cut withered. The Finance hearings ended on December 10, against Byrd's implicit threat while Kennedy was alive that that would not happen in 1963. Johnson made assurances he had no reason to believe that he would keep the budget in balance in upcoming years. Opponents had lost their stomach for a fight—it would have been too disgraceful to JFK's memory.

On January 23, 1964, the committee approved the bill by a vote of 12 to 5, with Byrd and Gore joining three Republicans in voting no. In short order the bill was law. Senate passage came on February 7, in a 77–21 vote. The House and Senate bills were reconciled, and the final vote resoundingly in favor in both houses came on February 26. LBJ signed the bill into law that evening in the White House and spoke to the nation about it on television. Dillon went to Jackie's residence in Georgetown to make a gift to her, her young girl and boy, and the Kennedy library of four pens that the president had used to make the Revenue Act of 1964 become law.

The moment after the Senate passed the resolved tax-cut bill that afternoon, February 26, 1964, the Senate majority leader, Mike Mansfield, Democrat of Montana, introduced a motion to put JFK's second big bill, the civil rights bill, up for full Senate debate and a vote. Sixteen days before, this bill had passed the House. Ordinarily, on passing the House, such a bill would not be considered next by the full Senate, but by the appropriate committee in that body, namely the Judiciary Committee. However, segregationist Democrat James Eastland of Mississippi chaired that committee, and it was clear that Eastland was not going to let the bill out of his panel. Mansfield's maneuver faced a brief "mini-buster" (an aborted attempt at a filibuster) by Eastland's allies on the Senate floor. This went nowhere, and in March the bill was opened up for full debate. At that point, southern Democrats successfully mounted a filibuster, and it lasted three months. When the filibuster broke in June, the Senate passed the bill, the House concurred, and it was sent to the president. On July 2, Johnson signed the Civil Rights Act of 1964. Within seven and a half months of the assassination, both of the big bills, the tax cut and civil rights, were law. John F. Kennedy's legislative legacy was complete.

The legislative dramatics that attended the civil rights bill, immediately upon the passage of the tax cut on February 26, showed that the tax cut would have been mightily endangered had it not come first. Southern Democrats surely would have striven to kill the tax cut in a show of vindictiveness. The southerners gave a clue as to their attitude in the presidential election the following November. The overwhelmingly Democratic five states of the Deep South pledged their votes to LBJ's opponent, Senator Barry Goldwater, who had voted against the civil rights bill on libertarian grounds. It was the strongest showing ever in that region by a Republican. Aside from his home state of Arizona, the corridor from Louisiana to South Carolina represented the only states that Goldwater won.

Goldwater had voted against the Revenue Act of 1964 in the Senate in February. The reason he gave was peculiar. He said that he did not like the kind of tax cut that Kennedy had proposed, even though Kennedy's tax cut specifically addressed the problems Goldwater had identified in the tax system. As Goldwater wrote in a campaign pamphlet that January, "I believe an intense study of our entire tax structure would disclose better and more equitable ways. . . . The steep rate of progressivity in our individual income taxes is damaging to our nation as a whole. Rather than stimulating economic growth, it often acts as a brake on that growth, dampening individual initiative rather than stimulating it. The impact of sharply rising tax rates in the middle income areas . . . is particularly disturbing." He added, "I reject completely the Administration position that the income tax is most useful as a means to redistribute wealth according to politically conceived blueprints."[1]

It appears that Goldwater misinterpreted the JFK tax cut. He accepted the CEA members' inaccurate characterization of it as a Keynesian measure, even though in point of fact it was an across-the-board marginal rate reduction meant to ensure the individual initiative that drives economic growth. In any event, Goldwater said that should he become president, he would continually cut tax rates, as he cut spending.

Twenty-one Senate Republicans voted for the Revenue Act of 1964 and ten against. The yea-voting Republican senators included eastern stalwarts Jacob Javits of New York and Leverett Saltonstall of Massachusetts. Saltonstall's junior as senator from Massachusetts, the assassinated president's brother Edward M. Kennedy, also voted in favor of the tax cut, along with fifty-five fellow Democrats, versus eleven Democrats against. Democrats in favor included liberal torchbearers Hubert Humphrey and Eugene McCarthy of Minnesota, Birch Bayh of Indiana, and Paul Douglas of Illinois. Of the Democrats opposed, seven of the ten were from the South.

The *Wall Street Journal* editorial page summed things up this way, the day after passage: "After a year of labor, Capitol Hill has brought forth . . . what is reputed to be the biggest tax cut in our history. We hope it does all the splendid things that it is supposed to do. . . . It seems to us, that for the tax cut to prove beneficial rather than harmful or downright dangerous the government must make other changes. It is spending too much, it is still running heavy deficits, and it continues to try to keep money artificially easy. . . . We all may hope that the tax cut will work the advertised wonders. . . . It's just that wonder drugs can sometimes be unpredictable; unless handled with care, they can be either depressing or too stimulating for comfort." The *New York Times* in principle agreed: "The upsurge in demand touched off by tax reductions . . . may well distort and strain the advance that is already in progress. . . . Too much ebullience too soon could result in a big letdown later."[2]

The CEA under Johnson was entirely devoted to the tax cut, first its passage from December 1963 through February, and afterward to the matter of highlighting its beautiful results. But with Kennedy gone, the CEA was able to shift nearly all of its rhetoric in support of the tax cut to the demand side. In the January *Economic Report of the*

President, virtually all of the justifications of the coming tax cut were, unjustifiably, Keynesian. Those "income tax rates born of war and inflation . . . were designed to curb demand in an economy bursting at the seams," went the report. A line most assuredly written by Heller claimed that the tax cut "will send well over $11 billion annually coursing through the arteries of the private economy." Talk of aggregates and consumption, and of investment stimulated by demand, predominated over that of incentives, risk taking, and asset shift out of tax-protected vehicles. Dillon laid out his standard, much more supply-side understanding of the theory behind the task cut. Not that the American people at large were paying attention to such policy-shop debates.[3]

The tax cut as it became law took the twenty-four rates of the income tax down from the range between 20 percent and 91 percent to between 14 percent and 70 percent, phased in over two years. Most of the rate reductions would come in 1964 and the remainder in 1965. An additional bottom bracket was added so that low earners would be hit by progressivity less severely, and their standard deduction was increased. The AFL-CIO president, George Meany, said that the tax cut amounted to a 7.5-cent-per-hour wage increase for the average worker. The maximum corporate tax was cut from 52 to 48 percent, with larger cuts in the rates applicable to smaller companies. The reforms in the bill were minor. The only one of passing general interest was the removal of the 1954 provision that 4 percent of stock dividend income could be deducted from taxes owed.

The newspaper editorialists were onto something when they fussed about the "upsurge" affecting the economy as the tax cut became law in 1964. Since 1962, the economy had been expanding mightily, leaving the precedent of the 1950s in the dust. Overall economic output increased by 6 percent in 1962, nearly 4.5 percent in 1963, and another 6 percent in 1964 as inflation went to level. The bipartisan goal of the 1960 campaign of 5 percent growth was achieved. And then sustained: after 1964, growth averaged slightly over 5 percent through Richard Nixon's inauguration as president in 1969.

Postwar prosperity at last became deserving of the name. Sixteen million new jobs appeared in the immense economic expansion dating from early 1961 to 1969 (about 3.5 million had come in the Eisenhower years), which at 106 months in length was the longest in the nation's history, according to the calculators at the National Bureau of Economic Research (though data from the pre-1929 era remains spotty). Median family income went up at a pace 50 percent higher than in the previous eight years. The American people doubled their savings, while throngs of baby boomers went to college without taking out loans.

As for new businesses, they sprang up like crazy. Business formation had been in a holding pattern in the 1950s, with the rate of failures matching that of start-ups. This pattern was broken as the ratio of businesses opening up to those folding leaped by nearly a third. One benefit of tax cuts was the freeing up of capital to flow out of shelters and into the real economy. The likes of Ralph Lauren, Merv Griffin Enterprises, MasterCard, and Trader Joe's arose to carry forward the American dream. Silicon Valley in California became a hive of activity as the "traitorous eight" engineers, led by Robert Noyce, who had left Shockley Semiconductor in 1957, nurtured the modern start-up culture. In 1968, Noyce and partner Gordon Moore founded Intel, the microprocessor company that enabled the personal computer revolution and the Internet.

Silicon Valley experienced a phase change, a maturation in its identity and purpose in the passage from the 1950s into the 1960s. Initially, the Valley, as it developed under the auspices of Stanford University provost Frederick Terman, was a function of defense contracts. Defense money poured into technological start-ups like Shockley's. Typical products were such things as guidance systems for the Polaris missile, the successful launch of which JFK watched as one of his last acts as president in November 1963. As the 1960s moved on, defense contracting began to cede primacy to start-ups, like Intel, whose vision was the development and production of fantastically new computerized devices and products for the market at large. What Noyce and his colleagues were doing, as Tom Wolfe wrote in the 1980s, was preparing "a bolt into the future that would create the very substructure, the electronic grid, of life in the year 2000 and beyond."[4]

It is difficult to imagine that had tax rates not been cut, the venture-capital (a term that exploded in use after 1964) and start-up culture of the Valley and elsewhere would have materialized as it did. The new firms could actually now pay a decent salary, with precious venture dollars, without having nearly all of it confiscated by the taxman. Capital accumulation could proceed, in that the rate of return for the highest earners rose from 9 cents on the dollar to 30 cents—an increase of 233 percent and the difference between a 91 percent and a 70 percent top rate. As high earners kept more of their money, more broadly marketable risks could be taken and visions pursued.

Across America, prosperity bloomed. If John Kenneth Galbraith was worried in 1958, in *The Affluent Society*, that the country was going in too much for domestic accouterments, the elegantly packaged food and car tail fins, he had seen nothing yet. Automobile purchases went up by 60 percent in the 1960s, having increased barely at all in the 1950s. Americans put furniture and appliances into their spacious homes in the 1960s at three times the rate of the decade before. And leisure came into its own. Sales of sporting goods, hobby equipment, and pleasure boats easily exceeded that of the 1950s. As for philanthropy, giving by individuals and corporations to charity increased by about half, as it had in the 1950s, even as the value of the tax deduction for charitable contributions had been reduced by the tax cut.

In 1958, policymakers had been stunned that the nation was suffering a youth unemployment rate of 18 percent while the huge baby boom generation was still under working age. When that bumper crop of kids hit the workforce as teenagers, the nation could be staring at a "juvenile delinquency" (a 1950s catchphrase) problem of gargantuan proportions. In the mid-1960s, youth unemployment fell back to mid-1950s levels, about 12 percent, as the legion of baby boomers entered the workforce. The problem of juvenile delinquency was akin to that of poverty, when regarded in terms of John F. Kennedy's innovative economic policy. Great economic growth might have been enough to wipe both of them out, necessitating no further programs.

It cannot be said that Kennedy would not have pushed for a military draft in the context of an indeterminate war (one function of LBJ's Vietnam War draft was to mop up non-college-bound young men from the workforce and keep them occupied), or that he would have waited to see if the Great Society of welfare programs was really needed given good economic growth. These points remain speculative because the assassination cut his life short just as the successes that Kennedy knew his legislation would procure were materializing. What can be said is that economic growth was the result that Kennedy desired, and it came. It is highly likely that had he lived, Kennedy would have been most interested in letting economic growth run so that it brought about its fruits in fullness. Now to see if the progress, with its champion dismayingly belonging to the ages, would last.

Chapter 10

REGRESSION

Though Kennedy's tax cuts unleashed new prosperity, diligent attention was required to ensure that continued supply-side legislation supported the boom—and Lyndon B. Johnson would not provide that attention. Despite his loyal pursuit of Kennedy's goals, he never had his heart in the tax cut, and though he did masterly work in passing the legislation, he was essentially ignorant of the economics involved. As other matters took his attention, tax policy—and the economy—began to slip back to their old ways.

Johnson recognized that southern segregationists countenanced high tax rates because the economic slowness that flowed from them compelled white-dominated unions in the North to resist welcoming African Americans into the labor pool. In turn, Johnson realized that the economic growth that the tax cut would buttress would reduce the ranks of the segregationists to the true believers. The unions (whose stronghold was the North) would no longer practice their form of Jim Crow—the withholding of jobs and job training from African Americans—because there would be plenty of employment to go around. In an August 1964 phone call, LBJ pressed Chicago mayor Richard Daley: "You don't think that the average worker . . . is scared the Negro is going to get his job?" After demurring, Daley at last told Johnson, "No, because fortunately, we . . . haven't had too much unemployment. We've had it among the low, unskilled fellows, but we have been bringing into the skilled building trades Negro members, and this they appreciate very much. . . . I really believe that when it comes to the actual vote in November, the [average workers] will be concerned about the prosperity." Prosperity buoyed by the tax cut would be the balm for white Americans' apprehensiveness over civil rights. Any such pragmatic solution to racism was a boon to the president.[1]

When it came to the deeper economic aspects of the tax cut, namely its relationship to the fiscal/monetary policy mix, Johnson was clue-less. Aside from some prepared speeches (probably written by So-rensen) that spoke of "incentives," he demonstrated no ability to speak extemporaneously about the varieties of tax cuts and their differential effects, of the reasons why a marginal tax cut was preferable to both a nonmarginal tax cut and increased government spending—all things that his predecessor had put in words so eloquently. The economic judgment that LBJ made of the tax cut was that it was a short-term mea-sure, instrumental to his main purposes of getting elected in the fall of 1964 and carrying the nation forward on civil rights. He told Daley in that same August 1964 phone call that he thought that the "maximum benefit of the tax bill" would be "in this third quarter" of 1964, as the presidential election campaign was entering its high season.

The idea that the peak effect of a major across-the-board tax rate reduction would come a few months after it became law would have bewildered Wilbur Mills, Stanley Surrey, certainly John F. Kennedy, and all those who had been militating for tax cuts and reform in the recession-prone 1950s and early 1960s. The point of lowering the top rate by something like 30 percent, commensurate with similar rate cuts all the way down the scale, was explicitly not short-term, but long-term. Every recovery from the 1950s recessions had produced a nice blip upward in economic growth—1959's was 7 percent. The problem was that the recoveries fizzled and produced another reces-sion within twenty-four to thirty-six months, with structural unem-ployment higher each time. The point of the tax cut was to ensure sustained economic growth, rather than a "quickie" economic boom-let that might have the collateral effect of helping out incumbents in the forthcoming election cycle.

Kennedy had spent the latter year and a half of his presidency, from the Yale commencement on, publicly and privately mulling over the policy mix and concluding with Robert Mundell that economic conditions called for a strong dollar and a fiscal flexibility that took the form of a marginal tax cut. But Johnson, hardly knowing what he was doing, immediately began undoing that work. Even before the year was out in 1964, he had pressured Federal Reserve chairman William McChesney Martin to loosen money so as to finance more federal spending. In November, he asked Martin for $500 million in Fed "surplus" to be deposited into the Treasury account, to "be a little help to me just like you were to Eisenhower back there in '59." Martin gave in and shifted the money to the federal government. LBJ told Dillon that he wanted to do "like Ike did . . . talked economy and then spent."[2]

The decline in federal spending from 1964 to 1965 was the first time that had happened since 1955. It was a feat not achieved again until 2010. Had the 1964–65 spending status quo been maintained, the extra revenue obtained from the tax cut would have easily over-whelmed government outlays—and further tax cuts would have been called for. This is the natural logic of the Laffer curve. If tax cuts result in more revenue, then taxes must continue to be cut, lest the govern-ment get large. In the 1960s, the revenue bonanza came not only to the federal government but to states and localities as well. The increase in general economic growth occasioned by the tax rate cut helped non-federal governmental entities rake in more receipts on their sales, property, and income taxes. One of the strategies that Senator Douglas of Illinois had adopted to push the tax cut through Congress in 1963 was to get state and local leaders to lobby their federal representatives for the bill. Douglas told them that the federal tax cut would result in over a billion dollars in new tax receipts at their levels. The estimate was surely correct. State and local revenues went up by 40 percent over the standard baseline, inflation plus population growth, from 1963 to 1969.[3]

After 1965, federal spending reversed trend and leaped. Expendi-tures were 36 percent higher in real, inflation-adjusted terms in 1968 than three years earlier. The reasons were Johnson's two big initiatives, the Great Society of domestic spending programs and the Vietnam War. Revenue was not the problem. Douglas Dillon had predicted that tax receipts to the government would be at maximal levels by 1967, given the tax cut. They were: 1967 federal receipts, in real terms, were 28 percent higher than in 1963, when Dillon had brought the tax-cut bill to the House. Over the whole 106-month boom, 1961–69, real federal receipts went up by 61 percent, greater than the economy's prodigious total of growth by 8 points.

Johnson notoriously called the Great Society—Medicare, Aid to Families with Dependent Children, and jobs programs—his "bride" and the Vietnam War his "bitch." They certainly were his two big spending ventures. A similar relationship obtained between the civil rights and tax-cut bills in the soul of LBJ. The former was his bride, that which he really cared about, and the latter—it was something that Johnson tolerated for instrumental reasons but had no strong attachment to, as events would soon demonstrate.

Though Johnson initially kept Kennedy's economic team on board, Dillon left after a year, as did Heller. In the summer of 1964, as the first historical recollections of the Kennedy administration were being made, Paul Samuelson was in a snit over claims about which adviser had been the real guiding light to the departed president. He had taken umbrage at a Harvard Business School commencement address that Dillon had given in June, in which Dillon explained that early on, Kennedy and his Treasury officials had settled on a tax cut as the main economic policy option that the administration would pursue. Dillon conceded that it had taken time to get the rate reduction prepared and for the right political moment found for it to be introduced, but held that his department and the president were of one accord from 1961 on that a tax cut like the one that came in 1964 was a necessity.

Samuelson wrote to Dillon to complain about this version of events and then set down his disagreement in an official oral history inter-

view with the John F. Kennedy Library. He said that the recommendation in Stanley Surrey's taxation task force report of December 1960
for a comprehensive reduction in rates in concert with tax reform was
supposed to be a temporary tax cut. "No permanent massive tax
cut"—that was how he remembered his own advice to the president,
and he thought that Surrey had agreed with him. Heller (whom *Look*
magazine was calling "Mr. Tax Cut") added, "There was really no
thinking, on the part of anyone, including us, of a permanent tax cut,
early in the game." Heller's colleague on the CEA, James Tobin, said,
"I was for a large temporary tax reduction all through this period."[4]

No matter this testimony, there remains no evidence that Stanley
Surrey, Wilbur Mills, Norman Ture, or, for that matter, John F. Kennedy, ever saw their final plans for across-the-board rate reductions as
anything but permanent. In Surrey's 1960 report, there was an option
for a temporary tax cut, but the reason given was that such a measure
would buy time for the real thing, the permanent tax cut. Kennedy
could not have been clearer in places like the Economic Club of New
York that he was "not talking about a 'quickie' or a temporary tax cut."
Rather, as he said to that audience in December 1962, "This administration pledged itself . . . to an across-the-board, top-to-bottom cut in
personal . . . income taxes" that of necessity was to be permanent.

Sorensen weighed in on the debate in 1965 with the publication of
his bestseller *Kennedy*. This was a blow-by-blow study of all of JFK's
major decisions, from the perspective of this ultimate insider, Kennedy's chief speechwriter and intellectual sparring partner and the
White House counsel.

Sorensen did a very able job in his considerable section on the germination of the tax cut, pointing out that it was Surrey's plan all along,
that Dillon had supported Surrey and keeping the dollar strong against
gold while the CEA plumped for spending and the temporary tax cut.
Sorensen implied that the CEA and Samuelson had voiced the view,
before August 1962, that they wanted the permanent rate cuts as long-

term policy after their short-term policy was implemented. The problem with this is that no evidence has ever turned up that the CEA or Samuelson, prior to JFK's tax cut speech of August 13, 1962, when the president announced his decision in favor of the Surrey plan, firmly advocated tax rate cuts in the long run. The few examples would include occasional remarks from Heller in the 1950s that he could consider such a thing, but even then he stressed the need to keep the current rate structure.

Beyond Sorensen, the recollections of Kennedy's CEA circle as of the early LBJ years made it clear that these advisers never had their heart in the tax cut that actually came, that of the Revenue Act of 1964. Their preference (as the *Economic Reports of the President* had consistently made plain) had always been for a temporary tax cut, so that the revenue-raising power of the government could be preserved for human-capital and social-welfare spending programs. This preference lived on in the LBJ administration, especially once Tobin's protégé at Yale, Arthur Okun, became a CEA member in 1964. Okun would praise Heller for having "carried the ball" for the Kennedy tax cut, conducting "the biggest course in . . . macroeconomics ever presented" by speaking to the press and the public about the "output gap" and the need for a "constructive deficit."[5]

With Okun in place in the administration (and Samuelson still writing policy memos), Johnson fondly recalling the political economy of 1959, and federal expenditures engorged, the pressure for a tax increase welled up, no matter the success of the 1964 tax cut. In 1968, it came: a 10 percent surcharge on income tax liability, delivered by Congress and signed by LBJ in June. Whatever you owed on your tax form, after all the calculations were made, it had to be upped by 10 percent at the end.

Thus did JFK's snubbed economic progressives ultimately get their wish, their whole economic policy, enacted in the 1960s. They got their temporary tax cut: the 1964 tax cut, though made law with no expiration, functionally was temporary after the surcharge of 1968. They got to write the history: the story retailed by Samuelson, Heller, Okun, and others that the 1964 tax cut was demand-side and the product of the CEA became the standard interpretation for fifty years. They got their stimulus and infrastructure spending, first under JFK himself in 1961 and 1962, and then after 1965 from LBJ in an even bigger way. And they got to kill off the policy mix, that alien idea of the Europeans and Robert Mundell: inflation, nil in 1964 and 1965, bounded up a point a year and hit 6 percent in 1969, as the Fed lowered real interest rates, ending the strong-dollar policy that had held since July 1962.

Just as Samuelson and the CEA had expected and desired, inflation served as a tax increase. Cost-of-living increases in pay put earners into higher income tax brackets. The policy mix that Kennedy had made in defiance of his Keynesian advisers, the revolution in economic thinking of sound money and reduced tax rates that JFK had carried high in the second half of 1962 and throughout 1963, proved, like Camelot of old, a brief and shining moment. It was consigned to the ages by 1968.

The assassination of November 1963 had provided an enormous short-term boost to the cause of the tax cut. It was fatal to it in the long term. The assassination was so shocking that the opponents of Kennedy's legislative agenda had to submit on at least one pet Kennedy goal out of due respect to the slain leader. The obvious choice was the tax cut. And once that was enacted, all leverage was lost on blocking civil rights. In the long term, however, Kennedy's absence after 1963 deprived the tax cut of its principal exponent, articulator, and enforcer. The cerebral tone that Kennedy brought to the question of the tax cut; his commitment to thinking through the real economic effects of a tax rate cut while unencumbered by the intellectual paradigms of university economics; the supreme social standing that he had in common with Dillon and Dillon alone; and the native ambition that Kennedy possessed that compelled him to solve the economic growth problem of his day had constituted the reason and credibility behind the administration's commitment to seeing the tax cut through. With Kennedy gone, the mechanism of the tax cut that had kept the logic keen and the motive force strong was gone too, no matter the phenomenal quality of the prosperity that it unleashed.

Johnson did not grasp the obvious point that, at 70 percent, the top rate of the income tax was still high, almost absurdly high. Of course cutting it (and other rates) to somewhere comfortably below 50 percent would have prompted more noninflationary production. Who focuses on sharply profitable activity to the exclusion of tax shelters, or idle leisure time, when the reward is 30 cents on the dollar? Surely very few of us.

Yet here was LBJ raising the top rate to an effective 77 percent via his 10 percent income tax surcharge. It was met with the boos that greeted much of everything that the president did in the annus mirabilis of 1968, the year of the Tet Offensive in Vietnam, Martin Luther King's assassination, and the "Yippie protests" at the Democratic National Convention in Chicago. Leftists called the surcharge a war tax. The likes of Howard Zinn, Noam Chomsky, Dwight Macdonald, and Betty Friedan signed a petition objecting to it. Johnson had quit on the presidency in any event, announcing in March that he would not be running for reelection that year, in the face of a challenge from a peace candidate, Senator McCarthy of Minnesota (who had voted for the tax cut in 1964). That same month, Johnson struck an agreement with the nation's major trading partners that they would refrain for asking for American gold, as they were entitled to at the long-standing $35-per-ounce price. The policy mix was moribund: the gold-dollar guarantee abrogated, and a tax increase on the books. A recession arrived in 1969, the first of four over the next thirteen years.

Republican Richard Nixon became president in January 1969, winning the election in 1968 that Johnson had declined to contest. He beat the Democratic nominee, Hubert Humphrey, an incumbent vice president as he had been in 1960. Nixon probably would have had to run against John F. Kennedy's brother Robert, had RFK not been assassinated the night of his primary victory in California in June. Whether Robert Kennedy would have cut tax rates as president, as his brother had, is an open question. RFK made an issue of closing tax loopholes in his brief campaign. Perhaps this meant he would have cut tax rates as well. His brother had been unremitting in making the link between loophole-closing and rate cuts—tax reform. Indeed, the only loopholes RFK approved of were those that could replace the social spending of the Great Society. As he told Merv Griffin on television in 1967, "I don't think . . . that the federal government can do it. . . . I think we have to . . . bring the private sector in, the businessman . . . make it attractive for them to invest in the ghetto. . . . They have to report to their officers and to their shareholders. I think you have to make it attractive through tax credits and . . . through tax write-offs."[6]

Nixon's economics bore no relation to JFK's or RFK's. This was possibly because he had absented himself from politics, for the only time in his adult life, during the years of the JFK tax cut's passage and implementation. In 1962, after he lost the race for governor of California, Nixon said that he was retiring from politics. He told the press, in one of his most famous lines, "You don't have Nixon to kick around anymore." For the next several years he practiced law. In 1968, as he unretired from politics, Nixon preferred not to discuss the economy, because it was surging under Democratic auspices—indeed achieving the 5 percent growth target that Nixon himself had specified in 1960 in the Compact of Fifth Avenue. (Nixon's issue of choice in the 1968 campaign was "law and order.") The Republican Party platform of 1968 reflected no new thinking on taxes. It spoke repeatedly of tax "incentives" that took the form not of marginal rate cuts but of exemptions, credits, deductions, and write-offs.

In office, Nixon completed the reversal of the Kennedy policy mix that LBJ had gotten started. On the fiscal side, he kept Johnson's income tax surcharge and supplemented it with an additional tax increase. This came care of the inappropriately named Tax Reform Act of 1969,

which raised the capital gains rate from 25 to 35 percent and introduced the alternative minimum tax (AMT) to hit those high earners
who took advantage of legal deductions to pay reduced proportions of
their income in taxes. There was an empty gesture toward tax-cutting
in the act. The rates that ran from 50 to 70 percent now applied only to
investment income, as opposed to salary income as well. Since most
high-salaried individuals also had considerable investment income,
the distinction was irrelevant. In passing the AMT, soon to be one of
the most loathed features in the tax code, and in keeping the surcharge
and raising the capital gains rate, Nixon revealed that he had absorbed
none of the previous fifteen years' worth of lessons on what high tax
rates can do to an economy—let alone to government revenue.

The signature "reform" of the act was the repeal of the 1962 investment tax credit—a dig at Kennedy and a threat to economic growth.
The rest of the so-called reforms were the exact opposite of reform:
two hundred pages' worth of complexity and new loopholes. The idea
that growth correlated to letting investment capital flow to natural
outlets, as opposed to tax havens, went by the boards. The big benefi-
ciaries were the tax-preparation and tax-planning industries. Wags
called the legislation "the lawyer and accountants' relief act." Nixon
signed it in December 1969, the very month that the eight-and-three-
quarter-year expansion of the 1960s came to an end.

On the monetary side, Nixon had a rare opportunity come before
him. He was able to appoint a Federal Reserve chairman in the first
year of his presidency, since William McChesney Martin retired in
early 1970. Nixon named his own economics confidant from the 1960
campaign, Arthur Burns, to replace him. Monetary expansion soon
exceeded the rate of the 1960s, when a huge economic boom was going
on. The Fed's "money stock" measure, M1, increased by 14 percent in
the essentially zero-growth years of 1969–71. M1's growth from 1962 to
1965, the golden years of the passage and implementation of the tax
cut, was also 14 percent—a shade under the 17 percent of real economic growth in that period.

The reversal of the JFK fiscal/monetary policy mix was a study in completeness by the second year of Nixon's presidency. The three tax increases undid the fiscal side. The first of these was Johnson's income tax surcharge, kept by Nixon. The second was the collection of increases from the Tax Reform Act, including the capital gains hike and the AMT. The third came by virtue of the inflation that was running at 5.5 percent per year. As individuals made more money to compensate for the increases in prices, their new earnings were taxed at the highest rate to which their previous income had been subject, or a higher rate if the new earnings threw them into a higher tax bracket ("bracket creep," as the odious phenomenon was called). The three tax increases reduced the take-home value of further profits and wages, stifling incentives and therefore growth, the great achievement of the 1960s.

The undue monetary expansion canceled the strong-dollar half of the JFK policy mix. As the Fed pumped up the money supply, goods and services rose in price. Since economic production was getting smaller on account of the tax disincentives, the problem compounded. Ever more money chased ever fewer things to buy. Then the price inflation itself morphed into a tax increase, via bracket creep, making for a vicious circle.

The recession that came with Nixon in 1969–70 was of the double-dip variety. The economy shrank for two quarters, bucked up a tiny bit, and then sank by 4 percent at an annual rate for one more quarter. As for inflation, consumer prices went up by 12 percent through the two years of recession. The new unemployed, whose ranks would swell by 2.5 million by 1971, depleted their savings and compensation dollars while prices were increasing at a rate not seen since 1951. Over the first twenty-one months of Nixon's presidency, beginning in the spring of 1969, economic growth, for a year and three-quarters, was cumulatively 0.36 percent—not 3.6 percent, but one-tenth of that level.

This is not to mention the unreality of even that growth, in that federal spending in real terms went up in Nixon's first three years nearly as much as it had in Kennedy's, about 10 percent. Vietnam was no longer serving as a pretext for the spending, in that American troop levels peaked in 1968 and fell sharply afterward. The reason for the spending was that Nixon built upon the domestic precedent of LBJ and funded federal agencies. Federal nondefense outlays went up a third, in real terms, in three years, 1969–72. Moreover, Nixon, along with Congress, was ratcheting up the regulation. During the recession, he authorized the creation of both the Environmental Protection Agency and the Occupational Safety and Health Administration.

What was Nixon doing? He was operating under the principles that had guided him as Eisenhower's vice president. In the 1950s, Republican orthodoxy had it that balanced governmental budgets were essential to private-sector growth. Given the budget shortfalls of the Vietnam–Great Society period, Nixon raised taxes. As for the monetary side, in 1960 (as he wrote in *Six Crises*), he believed that the Fed had been too tight, costing him the election. As president ten years later, he won loose money from his own Fed chairman. In the wake of the tax hikes and loose money, real economic performance was coming in at least as bad as in the recessionary periods of the 1950s—with the added nastiness of considerable price inflation. And when it came to spending, Nixon's former boss Eisenhower had had a weakness for it as well.

John F. Kennedy's advisers were not available to gainsay Nixon's departure from the growth economics of the 1960s, because those prominent in the media—Paul Samuelson and the veterans of the CEA—had never believed in the tax rate cut/sound-dollar policy mix to begin with. Among the genuine supporters, Douglas Dillon was preoccupied with cultural pursuits, serving as president of the Metropolitan Museum of Art; Stanley Surrey was back at Harvard Law School concentrating on specialist research; and Wilbur Mills had compromised with the rest of Congress in supporting the Tax Reform Act of 1969. The immense success of the 1960s had come and gone, but its lessons awaited a new generation.

Chapter 11

A NEW CAMELOT

The great Kennedy economic boom of the 1960s should have embarrassed the economics profession. Of the four combinations of the fiscal/monetary policy mix—loose fiscal policy with "high" (in JFK's phrase at Yale) or loose monetary policy, or tight fiscal policy with high or loose monetary policy—the one that JFK picked had to be imported from European sources at the Bank for International Settlements and had all of one advocate on American shores as of 1961, a twenty-nine-year-old Canadian staffer at the IMF named Robert Mundell who been spending time on the Continent and had a haircut that looked like Brian Wilson's. It was Mundell who had talked up strong money and expansionary fiscal policy at the IMF in 1961, his views represented in the BIS report of the following year. Dillon read about the debate and was impressed, and he used the logic to close the deal with Kennedy after the stock crash of May 1962.

Otherwise economics missed wildly on the great boom. Robert Solow's growth theory stressed government "investment" in human capital, in education and so forth. Kennedy made moves in this direction in 1961, and forecasts of a recession turned up. The neoclassical synthesis, in turn, was a moving target. Samuelson and company said it was loose money with high progressive taxes that produced "austere" (their term) budget surpluses—except that they approved of a deficit (loose money plus loose fiscal policy) if it came from spending on antirecessionary measures, post office construction, and so on, or from human-capital investment. In any case, JFK rebuffed it. As for the last option, tight money and high taxes, that was the bygone Eisenhower mix that guaranteed recessions.

As would not have surprised JFK in the least—his favorite aphorism was "victory has a thousand fathers"—economics wasted no time in taking full credit for the Kennedy boom. "Mr. Tax Cut" Walter

Heller was called the father of the "new economics," which became the subject of college courses and profiles in magazines and scholarly journals alike. Heller had, of course, abruptly suspended his neoclassical-synthesis/temporary-tax-cut/human-capital-spending principles to support the big, permanent Dillon tax rate cut when JFK strongly implied that he do so. Kennedy biographer Thurston Clarke believes that "Heller, like many in the administration, had fallen in love with Kennedy. It was a platonic affair, but romantic nonetheless, and his complaints [Heller got to be miffed that Kennedy never complimented him to his face, only to third parties, or asked him to join with the cool friends in a swim] sounded like someone bitching about a callous lover." Heller's successor at the CEA, Arthur Okun, gathered up all the credit for the boom himself, publishing a book on his policy behind the 1960s called *The Political Economy of Prosperity*.[1]

Economics, all the same, is a shrewd discipline, and everybody knew that Mundell had been the one who outlined the theory of the great 1960s expansion. A bidding war erupted for the services of this unimaginably brainy young MIT Ph.D., a bon vivant who friends observed could just as easily have served as a docent in any of the major European art museums. The University of Chicago, easily the top economics department in the country, won the bidding war. It installed Mundell as a professor in 1965, also making him editor of the department's flagship journal, and the top in the field, the *Journal of Political Economy*. The work Mundell did explaining the fiscal/monetary policy mix in 1962 was the first work listed in the citation for his Nobel Prize in Economics in 1999.

Yet even Mundell had not put the key final touch on the Kennedy policy mix. Expansionary fiscal policy had to be a cut in marginal tax rates—not all the other alternatives, not nonmarginal Keynesian "tax cuts," not government spending. That was JFK's own doing at the steady insistence of Dillon and Surrey. By the end of the 1960s, Mundell was making it clear that he grasped this point, that tax rate cuts had to be the fiscal aspect of his (now famous) fiscal/monetary policy mix. He also was aghast at two things: the reversal of the Kennedy policy mix in the late 1960s and the collusion in this dastardly deed on the part of his own economics profession, of which he was one of the most notable young members.

Mundell had been telling his colleagues at Chicago that the Kennedy mix had to be sustained and reapplied, but all he got were smiles and disagreement. Milton Friedman (with whom Mundell ran a seminar) said quitting the gold standard would be a great idea. Mundell got fed up and committed to making public statements that could jolt thinking back in the right direction.

Mundell's notable effort in this regard was a lecture in Italy in April 1971, a remarkable statement that both diagnosed what had happened in recent years and predicted the stagflationary 1970s, as well as showed the way out of that long flop as would eventually occur in the 1980s. Before a collection of the world's top macroeconomists, he made these remarks: "The 1968 tax increase . . . was a colossal blunder. . . . For, while money [was] expanding at a [high] rate . . . , the tax increase interposed a barrier to real expansion, causing the inflation rate to accelerate rather than decline. The tax increase cut into real expansion and increased inflation. . . . We got a depression without stopping the inflation." About Nixon's role in stoking the debacle, he said, "The 1969–71 recession was an economic catastrophe which cost more in wasted resources than the cumulative economic cost of the war in Asia, more than the entire GNP of 800 million Chinese." It happened because the United States had not pursued the *"correct policy mix* [Mundell's script put it in italics] of a reduction in the rate of monetary expansion . . . combined with a tax reduction"—the early 1960s solution that had won over JFK. "This would have stopped the inflation rate without causing a depression. . . . A whole year's growth . . . was lost."

Mundell reiterated what he had been saying now for a decade.

"The correct policy mix is based on fiscal ease to get more production out of the economy, in combination with monetary restraint to stop inflation. The increased momentum of the economy provided by the stimulus of a tax cut will cause sufficient demand for credit to permit real monetary expansion at higher interest rates." He added that tax cuts must "increase profits and raise the return to capital," which meant that they had to be tax rate cuts. And he said that the Fed was not to starve the economy of money, but rather understand that the right kind of tax cuts increase the *demand* for money. People (namely investors) will want to use money when tax rate cuts bring higher rates of return. "Growth of real output raises real money demand and abets the absorption of real monetary expansion into the economy without inflation." Mundell called out the "economic generals," the "prima donnas of economic academe," and the "economics profession" that was "far from guiltless" in shopping the bad ideas that had resulted in policy and hence the double-dip recession of 1969–70.

These economic generals and prima donnas of the economics establishment—how, precisely, were they "far from guiltless" in giving the JFK policy mix the shaft?

The most insidious example was the wide currency of the "Phillips curve," an economics diagram named after an economist from New Zealand by the name of A. W. Phillips, and drawn up in its classic form by Samuelson and Solow in 1960. Samuelson and Solow's Phillips curve suggested that there was a "trade-off" between unemployment and inflation. The more one rises, the more the other falls. The idea was that Federal Reserve looseness will make money so cheap that businesses will expand and hire workers, who in turn will become so cash-flush that their own spending will drive up consumer prices. Inflation, in this reckoning, is the price to pay for full employment. As inflation skyrocketed beginning in 1969, along with big jumps in unemployment, the Phillips curve somehow did not die when it was disproven in the 1970s, and it is alive and kicking in economic analysis in the twenty-first century. It has demonstrably been part of the belief system of Federal Reserve chairs and monetary expansionists Ben Bernanke and Janet Yellen.

As Samuelson wrote in yet another task force report, to LBJ in 1964, "The remarkable price stability which the U.S. has maintained over the past 6 years has in part been due to the high level of unemployment. One way of assuring a continuation of this price stability would be to tolerate continuing high unemployment. Like most Americans we reject this 'solution' to the problem of inflation." Samuelson recommended loose, preferably non-gold-based monetary policy to prime the economy, coupled with a regime of government-monitored if not government-enforced "controls" that compelled businesses not to raise prices (and workers not to take large wage increases). Via the Phillips curve, loose money would bring both jobs and inflationary pressures, but with price controls, those pressures would not become a reality in the form of actual higher prices.[2]

Kennedy and even LBJ never really went in for the controls—but Nixon did. Shamed by the sallowness of the nation's economy over the first two years of his administration, he did not reevaluate the situation and pivot to a new policy mix, as Kennedy had done. Rather, he kept the loose money and high taxes and set up an executive apparatus that effectively outlawed price increases. This was the signal to buddy Arthur Burns to keep gunning the money supply in the hope of boosting jobs. Burns had no choice, unless he wanted to take the heat from Nixon. As Burns wrote in his diary, "The White House staff has formulated a plan to blame the Fed if [the price controls] turn out to be a failure. The argument will be that the Fed failed to permit a sufficiently rapid growth of the money supply, and this, so the argument would go, [would be] responsible for the failure of the economy to recover as expected. The President himself was organizing a campaign . . . to his financial supporters on Wall Street [to] write me . . . and urge a more expansive monetary policy."[3]

The Nixonian Phillips-curve logic was that loose money would produce inflationary pressure and thus economic growth and employment, but the inflation would never materialize in consumer prices because raising prices was being made illegal. It was quite a gambit. Mundell was cool to it. "The idea that monetary acceleration necessarily increases employment," he said in Italy, "is one of those tired clichés that have . . . , by repetition, become elevated into a dogma. . . . [The] idea remains rooted in the psyche of . . . especially governmental officials, and part of the economics profession. . . . In the United States in 1970, the money supply expanded at a rate [upwards] of 12 percent, but unemployment jumped from 4 percent to 6 percent while prices continued to rise at . . . 5 percent. This occurrence alone should wake people up."[4]

The Nixon administration "woke up" in 1971 by doing something essentially unprecedented in American economic history. After a weekend of confidential meetings of his economic team at Camp David (the presidential retreat in Maryland), Nixon announced on August 15, 1971, that he was ending the dollar's link to gold altogether. From that moment on, the United States would not redeem the dollar for $35 or any price, even to foreign monetary authorities who had had the right since the Bretton Woods agreement of 1944 to exchange their dollars for gold on demand. As he made the announcement on Sunday-night television, Nixon said that he was throwing in an extra tax on imports for good measure—another step away from John F. Kennedy, the free-trader.

Officially, a weird little boom occurred. Growth soared for about two years. From 1971 through mid-1973, the nation's output as recorded by the government statistics went up at a 5.8 percent rate. Inflation shrank from 6 percent to 4 percent (the price control staff of two hundred agents could not catch everything). And the stock market filled up, with the Dow industrials nosing over 1,000 again.

It remains a common convention in economics and history today

to date the end point of postwar prosperity at 1973. President Barack
Obama's CEA chair Jason Furman did this characteristically, speaking
of "the golden age of 1948 to 1973." Such talk implies that the early
1970s (which encompassed the double-dip recession that held through
1970) were not a departure from the economic path of the real boom
years of postwar prosperity, the 1960s. Economist Alan Reynolds, one
of the supply-siders in Ronald Reagan's circle in the 1980s, has pointed
out the fallacies of considering 1973 the final year of postwar prosperity. Reynolds has noted that personal incomes went up in real terms in
the early 1970s only because prices were controlled. However, there
was less and less to buy—producers were conniving to withhold
product in expectation of the collapse of Nixon's controls. The controls
did in fact collapse over the next two years, inflation doubled to 11
percent, and any savings that earners had accumulated, as supply was
constrained through 1973, evaporated. Nineteen seventy-three was no
peak year. The 1960s, specifically the years in the wake of the JFK tax
cut, were the acme of postwar prosperity. This great era ended defini-
tively with the LBJ-Nixon transition, the abandonment of the JFK
growth model, and the brazen new attempts at federal management
of the economy.

Reynolds, twenty-seven years of age in 1971, and a former University of California economics student, made his writing debut in a
cover article for William F. Buckley's *National Review* in September
1971. "The Case Against Wage and Price Control" laid bare the administration's economic confusion, showing how Nixon met each new
failure in economic policy with a further expedient. It cited the influence, even within the Nixon administration, of liberal economists
Paul Samuelson and John Kenneth Galbraith. The article reflected implicitly the JFK policy-mix perspective. As Reynolds wrote, "It was the
government itself that brought on the current crisis through excess
monetary creation, oppressive taxation, and bureaucratic self-
indulgence." In that year when the United States went off the gold

standard, absorbed a tax increase, saw government spending boom, and experienced frightful expansions of the federal bureaucracy, Reynolds and Mundell represented the beginning of the renewal of John F. Kennedy's economics that would become realized a decade hence, in the Reagan years.[5]

Mundell found a sidekick at the University of Chicago. This was Arthur B. Laffer, the Yale undergraduate of 1962 who had witnessed JFK's commencement address that outlined the new fiscal/monetary policy mix. Laffer was now a University of Chicago business faculty member, on leave as chief economist at Nixon's Office of Management and Budget in 1970–72. As a scholar, he had been doing abstruse work exploring the difference between the "income effects" and the "substitution effects" of governmental policy. He concluded that marginal tax cuts—cuts in tax rates—held far more potential to expand the economy than nonmarginal ones. The reason was that marginal tax cuts had double the effect. Not only did they increase an earner's income (which nonmarginal cuts did as well), but they made earning more money more remunerative. An earner would no longer "substitute" earning for leisure (or nonearning) to the same degree after a marginal tax cut as before. Laffer was also studying currency "regimes"—specifically how currencies anchored in gold see a greater proportion of financial activity dedicated to real economic purposes (the production of goods and services), as opposed to speculation in currencies themselves.

Laffer was coming upon the policy mix of the late, great 1960s boom and talked about it with Mundell continually. In Washington, D.C., in the early 1970s, Laffer discussed these ideas with his boss, George P. Shultz; with his Chicago acquaintance Donald Rumsfeld (who held various positions in the administration); and with Treasury Secretary William E. Simon. But his most apt pupil was Jude Wanniski, a columnist with Dow Jones & Co.'s political weekly, the *National Observer*. Wanniski's beat was politics; he had no experience in economics. Given that Nixon was making news repeatedly with all his economic moves, Wanniski had to brush up on his economics. He called Laffer, the two became fast friends, and by the time of Wanniski's promotion to the editorial page of the *Wall Street Journal* (also under Dow Jones & Co.) in 1972, he had become a "supply-sider"—a term he himself would coin in 1976.

In May 1974, Wanniski met Mundell at a conference in Washington that Laffer had organized at the American Enterprise Institute. The timely subject of the conference was "the phenomenon of worldwide inflation." By 1974, the Nixon administration had despaired of trying to control prices, the oil-exporting nations had tripled the price of a barrel of petroleum from just over $3 per barrel to over $10 on the instruction of New York investment banks, and inflation was running in the double digits globally. Mundell explained the cause in his talk at the conference. Since the nixing of the international gold standard in 1971, at the behest of the United States, "confidence in currencies in general declined and a shift out of money and financial assets commenced." He put up a chart showing that a range of commodities limited in supply by the earth's geology were soaking up all the excess money and then some, as investors scrambled for hedges against currencies, the dollar in particular. Going up at a greater rate than oil were cotton, rice, sugar, and of course gold.[6]

Wanniski wrote an article about Mundell and Laffer's monetary views for the *Journal* the next month. In December, he did a piece on the pair's fiscal views. The title was "It's Time to Cut Taxes." Wanniski wrote that Mundell, in concert with Laffer, "believes that inflation and unemployment are separable problems and that to combat them distinct policy instruments are required. He believes that tight money should be used to combat inflation, while . . . lower taxes . . . can be used to combat the recession in a way that also works against inflation." Mundell's recommendation was a "$30 billion tax cut [that] would adjust income tax brackets across-the-board." Without specifying it by name, here was the John F. Kennedy policy mix that Mundell had first forwarded in policy debate in 1961, presented anew for the inflation-recession conditions of the 1970s: monetary restraint coupled with a marginal tax cut. The magnitudes were identical. JFK had introduced an income tax rate reduction of some 30 percent; $30 billion in 1974 represented 30 percent of federal income tax receipts from the previous fiscal year.[7]

The idea of reviving of the great 1960s policy mix was starting to get some traction, presented on the opinion page of the *Wall Street Journal*. The Gerald R. Ford administration, which had succeeded Nixon's in August, was showing interest. The week that "It's Time to Cut Taxes" appeared, Laffer met with Rumsfeld, now chief of staff to the president, and his assistant Dick Cheney. Rumsfeld and Cheney were considering taking the tax-rate-cut advice to heart, but the $30 billion number was high. Laffer, drawing a curve on a napkin, said that they need not worry. A well-designed tax cut could raise revenue, not lose it, just like in the 1960s. Laffer had drawn his curve many times before in the classroom. In his 1978 book *The Way the World Works*, Wanniski popularized the story of Laffer's sketching it for Rumsfeld and Cheney in December 1974.

Several weeks later that month, Mundell went to the White House to join other top economists, including Walter Heller, in a meeting with administration officials. He again put forth a "complete reversal of existing policy mix calling for massive $30 billion tax cut and tight monetary policy," as the notes from the day recorded it. Heller suggested "big tax cuts for stimulus to generate jobs, output, and profits" while staying "relatively sanguine about underlying inflation pressures." Mundell and Heller were remaining true to their early 1960s selves. Mundell wanted the fiscal/monetary policy mix that he had presented to the IMF and got before JFK's eyes via Douglas Dillon. Heller wanted a nonmarginal tax cut (probably along the lines of the exemption-upping bill proposed by Senators Edward Kennedy and Walter Mondale the previous April) and thought the dollar not a problem—the CEA's position from its reports in 1961 and 1962. Heller also said to "use fiscal revenues created by output gains to cover tax cuts and spending programs (repeat early 1960s)." He was on record as believing in the principle behind the Laffer curve, namely that tax cuts can raise revenue. The administration committed to a minor and decidedly nonmarginal move, a $200 rebate on taxes paid in 1974.[8]

At the White House, Mundell said that his was "more pessimistic than the consensus outlook." He characterized the current economic downturn as the "steepest recession since the 1930s with buildup of a high level of chronic unemployment." He was referring to the appalling recession that somehow was encompassing all of 1974, at sixteen months and lasting into 1975 the longest since the Great Depression. By the fall of 1974, the number of unemployed exceeded that of the double-dip recession of 1969–70, ultimately hitting 8.4 million in 1975, a total 60 percent greater than the peak of four years before. It was shades of the late 1950s, only more severe, this "buildup of a high level of chronic unemployment," words that could have been spoken by Michael Harrington. The stock market, for its part, was mimicking not the 1950s but the 1930s. In December 1974, the Dow industrials hit a level 45 percent below the 1973 peak, a drop unlike anything since the Great Depression. All the while inflation was powering beyond all peacetime precedents. Consumer prices rose 6 percent in 1973, 11 percent in 1974, and then 9 percent in 1975—a cumulative total of 29 percent in three years. The 8.4 million unemployed had to cope with not only the loss of a paycheck but price increases that stood to dissipate savings with rapidity.

The cost of the reversal of the John F. Kennedy policy mix was becoming inescapable. The relentless Federal Reserve expansionism, abetted by the abandonment of the gold standard, filled up the price level, ensuring not only sticker shock at the store on the part of the nation's shoppers but a massive transfer of private wealth to the government via the tax increases inherent in bracket creep. This in turn stifled incentives, making economic growth impossible, prompting historic layoffs. Loose money and high taxes—the opposite of JFK's policy mix—had cemented into the norm in the Nixon-Ford era. As of 1975, the nation had two double-dip recessions in the context of a bewildering inflation to show for it. The few voices reminding the nation of the secret of the success of the 1960s, of postwar prosperity, were not as yet numerous and influential enough to affect policy, but they were gathering.

Jack French Kemp was perhaps an unlikely heir to the Kennedy policy mix, even with his initials. This JFK had risen to fame in the 1960s far from the world of political economy, as a football player, a quarterback for the San Diego Chargers and Buffalo Bills of the American Football League for the full ten years of that league's existence, 1960–69. As a football player, Kemp relished working on a team, getting hit, winning, and being one with especially his African American teammates. In his years as a professional athlete, he still made sure to nourish his interests in politics and ideas. He read in political economy and interned for Ronald Reagan in California, where Kemp had grown up, worked in the family business, and gone to college. Kemp entered the House of Representatives in 1971, the year after he retired from football.[9]

The Buffalo area, in particular the steel mills in Kemp's district set around the big Bethlehem Steel plant in Lackawanna, New York, went through especially difficult times in the 1970s. The problem stemmed from the way that the high inflation of the period mixed with the tax code. Capital-intensive manufacturing companies counted their equipment purchases against taxable revenue. The tax code required companies to take years to write off such purchases in nominal dollars, with no accounting for the fact that inflation was making nominal dollars ever more worthless. Furthermore, the big jumps in consumer prices made it difficult for companies to give their workers real raises, because of bracket creep. The result was that industry became reluctant to modernize and keen to lay off workers.

Kemp "didn't come to Congress, really, with a well-formed economic philosophy," an ally of his in Washington, Republican Representative Vin Weber of Minnesota, recalled. "He came to Congress representing a district that was going through very great difficulties and he realized he didn't have anything to go back and tell them. So he started studying economics and trying to come up with something positive to say to a blue-collar town that was in decline, as most manufacturing towns were at the time. And this set him on the course."[10]

In 1974, Kemp introduced a bill in the House that enabled companies to take write-offs on equipment purchases more quickly, the same thing that had gotten business behind Kennedy's tax proposal of 1962. President Ford and the Democratic Congress rebuffed him, fearing a revenue loss that would increase the deficit and thus inflation. In Kennedy's and Dillon's logic of a dozen years earlier, however, write-off reform would stabilize the dollar and counter inflation, by drawing more money, including foreign money, into investment in American businesses. Kemp redid his bill in 1976, so that in addition to the business tax cut, it also specified a 10 percent reduction in all rates of the income tax. The two prongs of the original JFK policy mix, a strong dollar and tax rate cuts, were finding a reprise in the legislation of the new JFK—Kemp.

Jude Wanniski wrote about Kemp's efforts in the *Journal* and pointed out the connections to the original JFK. "Clearly the Kennedy rate cuts [of the 1960s] were successful gambles," Wanniski wrote. "Kemp . . . has been the only Washington politician aggressively pushing the Mellon/Kennedy concept—around which he designed a tax-cutting Jobs Creation Act. But at every turn, he has been shot down by the Treasury tax people who reject his assertions that a lowering of rates would expand Treasury revenues. The hard analysis that went into the Kemp assertions, ironically, was provided by the same economist who helped work out the Kennedy tax cuts, Norman B. Ture." Ture, who had worked on depreciation reform on congressional staffs in the 1950s, been a member of Stanley Surrey's taxation task force for the JFK presidential transition, and assisted Wilbur Mills on Ways and Means as the Kennedy tax bills got prepared, was now a consultant advocating the Kemp plan.[11]

The 10 percent reduction in income tax rates that Kemp proposed in his 1976 Jobs Creation Act actually amounted to no real tax cut at all, given the effective tax increases of recent years. Bracket creep had become such an extreme phenomenon in the inflationary 1970s that nonstatutory tax increases were coming in at several percentage points every year. Kemp's 10 percent cut of 1976 would have restored the income tax status quo of the early 1970s. If tax rates were to be reduced such that people kept as much of their income as when Kennedy's tax cut was in place in 1965, rates would have to go down by more than 10 percent—assuming that inflation did not continue to gallop in the years after 1976. The problem affected the middle and working classes, the base of Kemp's congressional district, as acutely as any of the rich. Hence the across-the-board nature of his tax cut.

The numbers bore out the problem clearly. From 1968 through 1975, consumer prices went up a total of 55 percent. Any series of raises that an earner got over this period was additional income subject to the highest tax rate to which his or her previous income had been subject, if not a higher rate. In 1968, somebody making $10,000 a year (about $68,800 today) paid taxes at 14, 15, 16, 17, and 19 percent, for after-tax pay of about $8,658 (or $59,575 today). An inflation-matching series of raises of 55 percent through 1975, increasing pretax income to $15,500, would subject this earner to all the previous tax rates, plus rates of 22 and 25 percent on most of the additional income. Take-home pay after taxes (including increased standard deductions enacted in the 1970s) would be $13,140 (about $57,875 today), meaning that taxes went up by 70 percent while raises totaled 50 percent. As the numbers worked out, the raises would have to have been several points higher than the increase in the price level just to keep even against inflation and taxes. The effect was sharper on those who succeeded in earning more.

In these circumstances, it became difficult for businesses to grant workers raises that kept up with inflation. Doing so meant devoting ever more profits to costs—while workers who got the raises saw no improvement in living standards. Bracket creep combined with minuscule production-cost write-offs was a brutal reality for employers and employees in the 1970s: sales morphed into taxable profits, and workers had to be extra-compensated just to stay even. Companies became loath to maintain (let alone expand) operations, and workers needed overtime. Investment funds and personal savings departed from this environment and bailed out to hedges such as oil, gold (legal for Americans to hold again in 1975), commodities, and land. These tangible assets paid no dividend or interest that could be taxed every year. Since they were sharply limited in supply by geology, they went up in price at a rate greater than inflation.

A great contradiction arose: the economy was *stagnating* (actually shrinking by 3 percent in 1973–75) in the context of severe *inflation*. A British term from the 1960s combining these two words gained currency in the United States. America was experiencing "stagflation." According to the Phillips curve, this was impossible, in that inflation decreases unemployment. But as Mundell had said in Italy in 1971, "The United States [does] not have inflation-immune tax structures." Inflation made earners who tried to keep up with it face higher tax rates, transforming more and more private income into government revenue. This decreased the incentive to work in the first place, so government revenue flagged as economic growth stopped. Federal receipts, in real terms, were no greater in 1975 and 1976 than they had been in 1969. In 1975, inflation ran at 9 percent (a level unheard of since the Korean War), as unemployment hit 9 percent—1.5 points higher than the worst mark of the 1950s.

When he was a staff economist on the John F. Kennedy Council of

Economic Advisers, Arthur Okun adopted a term from weather reporters who combined the summer temperature and humidity numbers into a "misery index." Okun added up the unemployment and
inflation percentages and called the result the same thing. In the 1960s,
his misery index ran between 5 and 10. In 1965, when unemployment
was 5 percent and inflation 1 percent, it was all of 6. In the 1970s, the
unemployment/inflation misery index soared to extreme heights: 18
in 1975. Just like stagflation, Okun's index became a common point of
reference in discussions of the American economy in the 1970s. Stagflation, misery index, bracket creep—these unattractive terms, in the
Ford and then the Jimmy Carter years, characterized discussion of an
economy that traditionally had been spoken of in terms of the American dream.

The period of 1973 to 1975 was the worst recession since the Great
Depression—worse than 1957–58 and since eclipsed by 1979–82 and
2008–9. The sixteen months spent in recession were the most since
1933; the economy contracted in five out of eight quarters (the first
time that had happened since record keeping began in 1947); and the
private sector was 6 percent smaller in 1975 than in 1973. The conve-
nient explanation of the oil shock from Arabia—the big increase in the
price of a barrel of petroleum in the wake of the Yom Kippur War in
the fall of 1973—was vacuous. No matter its significance to the economy, oil was going up at no greater rate than dollar hedges such as
gold and other primary commodities. It went up about threefold from
1973 to 1975, the same as gold. In 1977, University of California economist Roy Jastram published a book called *The Golden Constant*, showing that sustained increases in commodity prices correlate not with
demand booms or supply problems, but with widespread interest in
defending savings against questionable monetary policy and the depreciation of the currency.

The group favoring a reimplementation of the John F. Kennedy policy mix that had been budding around Mundell, Reynolds, Laffer, and

Wanniski in recent years added a significant new member in 1975. Wanniski's boss at the *Wall Street Journal*, editorial-page editor Robert L. Bartley, declared himself curious about this heterodoxy, this cause that the *Journal* had opposed in the 1960s. Bartley arranged to meet every month with this group for drinks, dinner, and conversation at a restaurant near Wall Street called Michael 1, sometimes at other places, and with new company, including Laffer's young associates Charles Kadlec and Wendell Gunn. These dinners continued for several years, organized by investment-house manager Charles Parker.

The main talkers at the get-togethers were Mundell and Laffer. In 1992, in his memoir *The Seven Fat Years*, Bartley summarized the views that these two economists had put forth at Michael 1 and its successors. A "Mundell aphorism," as Bartley wrote in the book, was that "for every policy goal, you need a policy lever. . . . You fight inflation with monetary policy, preferably international and preferably with a commodity link, but in any event with tight money. And you fight stagnation, you stimulate the economy, with incentive-directed tax cuts. You find the highest marginal rates and cut them." This aphorism of the 1970s was akin to the policy mix that Kennedy had outlined in his 1962 Yale speech as an intriguing alternative to loose money and Keynesian budget policy, and that he would adopt later that summer and shepherd into practice for the remainder of his presidency. A key clarification that Mundell made at Michael 1 was that "tight money" did not mean undue restriction, but simply devoting monetary creation to the demands of the private economy, as opposed to helping government with its funding desires as well.[12]

The main point that Laffer stressed to Bartley at Michael 1 concerned the kind of tax cut that had to be made, given the conditions of stagflation. Laffer used the economics jargon that he had become accustomed to at the University of Chicago. There are both *income* effects and *substitution* effects to any tax cut, he told Bartley. A nonmarginal or Keynesian tax cut—one that increases exemptions or deductions, involves a rebate against taxes paid, or cuts lower rates in the progressive tax code but not the upper ones—has an income effect. People get to keep more of the income they are already earning. However, such a tax cut provides earners with little or no incentive to enhance their economic activity, to make more money, because further earnings remain unaffected by a nonmarginal tax cut. Income at the margin stays dunned at the same high rates.

In contrast, marginal tax cuts—tax rate cuts, the kind that Kennedy had proposed and won in the 1960s—have both income and substitution effects, Laffer explained. With a cut in every rate of the income tax, individuals get to keep more of the money they are already earning—the income effect. But in addition, individuals get to keep a greater proportion of any additional income that they may make. A marginal tax cut also has a substitution effect, whereby earners "substitute" economic for noneconomic activity, given that new economic activity pays more on account of the tax rate cut. Across the economy, given a tax rate cut, people will do things like pick up more hours at work, give up government benefits for a wage-paying job, and pull money out of a hedge investment in gold or oil to start a business. A nonmarginal tax cut only has the income effect, but a marginal tax cut has both the income and the substitution effects, Laffer told Bartley. In an economy racked by stagflation, why not go for the more powerful kind of tax cut?

John F. Kennedy had made similar points, such as in his legendary 1962 speech at the Economic Club of New York. Kennedy said that "if we do not take action," namely, pass a "top-to-bottom cut in personal and corporate income taxes," then "those who have the most reason to be dissatisfied with our present rate of growth will be tempted to seek shortsighted and narrow solutions—to resist automation, to reduce the work week to 35 hours or even lower, to shut out imports, or to raise prices in a vain effort to obtain full capacity profits on under-capacity operations. But these are all self-defeating expedients which can only restrict the economy, not expand it." A tax-rate cut, Kennedy was certain in 1962, as Laffer was in the 1970s, would prompt people to bound into new economic activity—instead of making a priority of protecting income streams that they already had.

It took a while for Bartley to be won over by such arguments. It had been a verity of the editorial page at the *Journal* for years (including during the battle over the JFK tax cut in the previous decade) that taxes were not to be cut unless the budget was in balance. This was far from the case in 1975–76, when the federal deficit zoomed up to 4 percent of national economic output, 45 percent higher than the Vietnam War/Great Society–era maximum. Bartley stayed pensive and commissioned Walter Heller, of all people, to write a column for his page. But he did come around after about two years' worth of drinks, dinner, and all the talk at Michael 1.

In March 1977, Bartley ran a lead editorial under the headline "Tax the Rich!"—and the *Journal* passed into a new era. From this point on, the main, unsigned editorials, those by implication carrying the voice of the editor, argued for tax rate cuts and dismissed concerns about short-term budget deficits. "You can't get rich people to pay more in tax *revenues* by raising their tax *rates*," the "Tax the Rich!" editorial asserted, the italics indicating that Bartley had been listening to Laffer. "If you raise rates, it becomes even more profitable for them to hire lawyers and accountants to find them loopholes, and the cost of this misdirected effort is a dead loss to the economy. Or they stop working entirely and dissipate their capital drinking champagne and sailing yachts, which is also a dead loss to the economy. Either way, they contribute less in tax revenues, and the burden of supporting government . . . falls on the middle class and poor." The editorial concluded, "Why not tax the rich by lowering the rates they face? . . . By all means, tax the rich! But do it right, and in this fashion lift the burdens of taxation from those who aren't rich."[13]

Again John F. Kennedy had made all the same points in 1962. To the Economic Club of New York he said, "The present patchwork of special provisions and preferences lightens the tax load of some only at the cost of placing a heavier burden on others. It distorts economic judgments and channels an undue amount of energy into efforts to avoid tax liabilities. It makes certain types of less productive activity more profitable than other more valuable undertakings. All this inhibits our growth and efficiency. . . . These various exclusions and concessions have been justified in part as a means of overcoming oppressively high rates in the upper brackets—and a sharp reduction in those rates, accompanied by base-broadening, loophole-closing measures, would properly make the new rates not only lower but also more widely applicable. Surely this is more equitable on both counts." Kennedy added in the same speech, "I am confident that the enactment of the right bill next year will in due course increase our gross national product by several times the amount of taxes actually cut. Profit margins will be improved and both the incentive to invest and the supply of internal funds for investment will be increased. There will be new interest in taking risks, in increasing productivity, in creating new jobs and new products for long-term economic growth."

The Kennedy arguments that Vermont Royster had been cool to in the 1960s were by 1977 the stated position of the editorial page of the *Wall Street Journal*, easily the nation's premier business newspaper, and also its largest newspaper by circulation. The revival in practice of the John F. Kennedy policy mix became a real possibility, in that the cause now had a prominent platform. The *Journal* would make the case for sound money and tax rate cuts nearly daily through the remainder of the 1970s and into the 1980s to its large and influential readership.

Meanwhile, in political haunts like the 1976 Republican National Convention, Wanniski and Laffer were trying to gin up interest among officeholders in an across-the-board tax cut of the size Kennedy had proposed in 1963, of 30 percent. Kemp picked up on the idea. In early

1977, he hired staffer Bruce Bartlett and told him, "We keep talking all the time about the Kennedy tax cut. Why don't we just replicate it? Let's get rid of all this baggage and just do a clean, straight duplication of the Kennedy tax cut." Bartlett changed Kemp's proposal from a 10 percent to a 30 percent reduction in all rates of the income tax. That summer, Kemp landed a Senate sponsor in Republican William V. Roth of Delaware. Roth's one condition was that the rate cut be phased in over three years, 10 percent the first year, 10 percent the second, and 10 percent the third. The Revenue Act of 1964 had rolled out the rate cuts over two years.[14]

Kemp-Roth, as the "10-10-10" marginal tax-cut bill became known, reaffixed the John F. Kennedy (and Andrew Mellon) growth model in Congress, as the nation was beset by an economic mess—stagflation— that was worse than the Eisenhower-era sluggishness and on par with the "forgotten depression" of 1919–21 (the subject of the remarkable recent book of that name by James Grant). Kemp-Roth was the lever for the fiscal side of the policy mix. On the monetary side, recommit- ment to a sound dollar, preferably one that was stable against the pri- vate price of gold, was the preference of the Michael 1 circle. Mundell cautioned—as he has been cautioning to this day—that money was not supposed to be "tight," as the Eisenhower people were trying to keep it in the recessions of the 1950s. Rather, while the Federal Re- serve was to be vigilant about money, it also had to increase the money supply vigorously when the economy was poised for major activity, as it would be given a big tax rate cut. Douglas Dillon's position during the JFK years was that marginal tax cuts would end the flight from the dollar, enabling the government to supply dollars in concert with the actual demand for them in the private sector. Economic growth would flow from tax rate cuts, and inflation would die off because money would head into investment as opposed to the price level and hedges against the dollar.

In September 1977, the Republican National Committee (RNC) en-

dorsed Kemp-Roth in its roster of official policy. The new leader of the
RNC, Bill Brock, had just been defeated for reelection for his Tennes-
see Senate seat. He was a victim of one of the serial electoral routs that
the Republicans had been suffering in the wake of the Watergate scan-
dal and the atrocious recession presided over by Nixon and Ford from
1973 to 1975. Brock noticed that Democrats had been framing Republicans as being anti-everything in recent years. "We were, at least in
perception, anti-women, anti-minority, anti-union, anti-black," he
said. "I was trying to create a different kind of party and it was a deliberate objective of getting women elected, minorities elected, young
people, blue collar, union. And we needed a catalytic agent. . . . Kemp,
with his big-tent approach and new ideas, could be that catalyst."
Kemp "talked about the income tax as something that affected every
individual. . . . So that became really attractive to me."[15]

As Brock made Kemp-Roth party policy for these reasons in 1977,
he perhaps unconsciously marked the transition point where the
Democrats ceased being the party of tax cuts and ceded this position
to the Republicans. After all the social tumult in the United States of
the late 1960s and early 1970s, the Democrats had become a party more
defined by its cultural wing, by critics of American history and institutions. The interest in economic growth that had animated Kennedy
and his party in 1960 had fallen from grace. Replacing it, in the Democratic mind, was an inclination to curb the natural processes of the
nation and its people, to subject the ways of American life to government oversight if not control.

In turn, that party stung by its reputation for being old-fashioned
and slow-moving, and shocked by the economic predicament of the
1970s, the Republicans, migrated to the position vacated by the Democrats. Leadership on the issue passed from the party of one JFK, Kennedy, to that of another, Kemp. The Republicans began to become the
party of tax cuts. To be sure, the process took time. Old-school, "green-
eyeshade" (Robert Novak's epithet) Republicans, such as Senators Rob-

ert Dole and Pete Domenici in the Reagan years, remained opposed to tax cuts and in favor of tax increases, on budgetary grounds. And as the politics of the Jimmy Carter, Ronald Reagan, and even Bill Clinton administrations would show, every time tax rate reductions became law in the 1970s through the 1990s, there was notable bipartisan support.

When Kemp-Roth came on the scene in 1977, its advocates adopted a new name for themselves. They became the "supply-siders." The year before, Alan Reynolds told Jude Wanniski that he had heard the former Nixon adviser Herbert Stein call the Wanniski crowd "supply-side fiscalists," whatever that quite meant. Wanniski liked the sound of it, but made a change. He said that what he was supporting was "supply-side economics." In 1977, the term became idiomatic in discussions of current events.

The contrast was to "demand-side economics." This was the policy that sought to "put money in people's pockets"—Laffer's income effect—by means of nonmarginal tax cuts, increases in government spending (as Kennedy had tried in 1961), and loose money from the Federal Reserve. Supply-side economics focused less on current income and more on what made people strive to improve themselves in life. Taxes were to be cut on current income, to be sure, but also on additional increments of income. This is what made tax rate cuts different from all other kinds of tax cuts—what made them the supply-side kind of tax cuts.

In addition—and this point is often forgotten or elided in commentary to this day—tax rate cuts alone did not define supply-side economics. A recommitment to a sound dollar had to accompany a tax cut. It was a policy *mix*. Money had to be sound, constant especially against gold and other major commodities. This would render unnecessary the protecting of savings against a declining dollar, prompting owners of accumulated resources to push into new economic ventures. The economic effect would be as large as that of any tax cut. Both halves of the policy mix relied upon each other. Tax rate cuts could spur new initiative only if people had confidence in the dollar. Confidence in the dollar could result in new initiative only if additional income was not to be confiscated by taxation.

The year of the tax cut turned out to be 1978, even if it was not at all one of sound money. President Jimmy Carter, a Democrat, who succeeded Ford in January 1977, was interested in reforming the tax code. He called the code "a disgrace to the human race" on account of its complexity and lobbyist-procured loopholes. Oddly, however, he wanted to close loopholes and raise the highest rates in the code, a double tax increase at the top. He advocated expanding the brackets at the bottom of the tax rate structure, so that lower earners were hit less by bracket creep.[16]

Carter's ruminations about the inadequacies of the tax code were pronounced enough to permit his lieutenants to say things that appeared to advocate the kind of tax reform that John F. Kennedy had championed. In 1977, Carter's treasury secretary, Michael Blumenthal, wrote to Congress, the "increase in receipts [of $54 billion from 1962 to 1968] was the result of both changes in legislation over the period and growth in the economy. Therefore, this history shows that receipts generated by six years of growth in the economy more than compensated for any revenue losses resulting from changes in legislation." Carter's budget director, Bert Lance, said that same year, "My personal observation is that as you go through the process of permanent tax reduction, that there is an awfully good argument to be made for the fact that the revenues of the government actually increase. . . . I think that has been proven. . . . I have no problem in following that sort of thing." And Walter Heller chipped in. Before a congressional committee in February 1977, he said of the Kennedy tax cut that "within one year the revenues into the federal treasury were already above what they had been before the tax cut. . . . Did it pay for itself in increased revenues? I think that the evidence is very strong that it did."[17]

With memories of the Kennedy tax cut starting to glow, Kemp-

Roth gained some legislative momentum. In 1978, several bills providing for the 10-10-10 tax rate cut popped up in Congress, each one
attached with riders saying that the rate cuts would be canceled if federal spending went up beyond certain levels. On several occasions,
the bills just about cleared majorities in the House and the Senate. It
was, however, certain that Carter would veto a revenue bill that did
not increase the progressivity in the income tax rate structure. As
Wanniski had written in one of his *Journal* opinion pieces, called "JFK
Strikes Again," "Jack F. Kemp . . . unabashedly gives credit for his
idea to John F. Kennedy. . . . It is not only baffling, but almost comical,
that Mr. Carter rejects this Democratic precedent while embracing the
tax rebate scheme adopted by Gerald R. Ford in 1975."[18]

The tax rate cut that did pass in 1978, and that Carter signed into
law that November, came on the capital gains side. In April of that
year, William A. Steiger, a young representative from Wisconsin
whom Laffer had been talking to, proposed a cut in the top capital
gains rate—the rate an individual pays on investment gains—from a
level that was effectively at 49 percent to 28 percent. The problem with
the 49 percent capital gains rate was that inflation had made it punish-
ing beyond belief. Even today the capital gains section of the tax code
does not make any provision for inflation. If you buy a stock at $100,
sell at $130 three years later, and inflation has been 30 percent in the
meantime, you have to pay taxes on that $30, even though it is a phan-
tom gain. You lose money (to the government) even as your investment stays even against inflation.

In the 1970s, this situation was becoming thoroughly outrageous.
Stocks were struggling even to be flat, and anytime a minimal real
gain was eked out and realized at sale, in came the capital gains levy
to take the whole gain and then some. After the 10-percent-range inflation of 1974–75, price increases came in at an annual rate of 7 percent from 1976 to 1978. Carter appointed a new Federal Reserve chair
in 1978 on Arthur Burns's retirement. G. William Miller kept up the

policy of loose money, with no rule whatsoever on following the price of gold, commodities, or anything hard and external. Investors became loath to put their money in the market or in start-ups, out of the necessity to have an inordinate gain just to break even against inflation and capital gains taxes.

All year long, Carter huffed that he was not going to cut a tax rate that mainly affected the rich—notwithstanding the fact that capital investment leads to jobs and wage growth. The president conceded to signing the bill containing the Steiger measure in October when faced with the popular congressional alternative: that or Kemp-Roth with spending caps. The Revenue Act of 1978 reduced the top capital gains rate effectively by 21 points, to 28 percent, as it expanded the brackets of the individual income tax. It was the closest approach to the tax policy championed by John F. Kennedy since 1964, though still a far sight from the comprehensiveness of the Revenue Act of 1964. Bartley's page wrote in the *Journal* that "the tax bill does not leave us in a state of total pessimism. For it's possible that looking back from, say, 1984, we will see this year's tax debate as the start of a sea change." That December, a month into the lower capital gains rate that he had steered into law, William A. Steiger died at the age of forty, the victim of a heart attack. In the final year of the stagflation decade, the cause of the John F. Kennedy policy mix, of the growth model also pioneered by Mellon in the 1920s and now called supply-side economics, presumably had its leader in Jack French Kemp.[19]

Chapter 12

THE REAGAN REVOLUTION

What was Ronald Reagan's position on Kemp-Roth and the policy-mix, growth-model legacy of John F. Kennedy? Kemp would decline to run for president in 1980, even for the New York Senate seat open in 1980 (won by obscure Republican Alfonse D'Amato), probably because for all his policy boldness, he was modest to a fault about managing his own political career. The Republican Reagan would win the presidency in 1980, cut tax rates along the lines of Kemp-Roth, secure a sound dollar, preside over a phenomenal and exceptionally long-lasting economic boom, and remain the most influential American political figure since Kennedy, well into the twenty-first century.

As an actor in Hollywood in the 1940s and 1950s, Reagan abhorred high tax rates because of their negative incentive effect. He spoke many times of his own aversion to success in Hollywood, because it meant giving to the government 91 cents of every marginal dollar earned. In 1962, he supported an across-the-board tax rate reduction spread out over five years that allies of Barry Goldwater were attempting to introduce in Congress independent of Kennedy's proposal. But in the speech that launched his political career, his remarkable hour-long oration in October 1964 in support of Barry Goldwater's presidential candidacy, "A Time for Choosing," a speech that Reagan had honed for years speaking on the circuit for General Electric, there was no mention of tax cuts or the problem of taxation in any but an oblique way. Perhaps this reflected embarrassment about the obvious success of the Democrats' big tax rate cut of 1964. The main themes of "A Time for Choosing" were alarms about the concentration of power in Washington and the threat of international communism.

As governor of California from 1967 to 1975, Reagan signed perhaps a dozen general revenue bills into law, the preponderance resulting in tax increases. His concern was for a balanced budget. In 1981, reporters Rowland Evans and Robert Novak reflected on Reagan's time as governor this way: "When he left office, the California tax system was far more progressive than he found it, with upper-income individuals, corporations and banks paying a markedly higher share of the state's revenue than they had [previously]. Had Reagan abandoned his old conviction that tax progressivity sapped initiative and growth? Not at all. He had been trapped. Unable to achieve or even seriously propose radical budget cuts"—largely because of federally mandated spending at the state level, on such Great Society programs as Medicaid—"Reagan had to search out new sources of revenue where available and easiest to obtain. This meant tax withholding and high progressivity of rates."[1]

When he ran for the Republican nomination for president against the incumbent Ford in 1976, Reagan made a major proposal for a tax cut—coupled with a huge spending cut. He proposed a 23 percent tax cut (without specifying what form it would take), offset by a whopping $90 billion reduction in yearly federal spending. The plan was to identify those areas of federal spending better handled by the states, eliminate that spending at the federal level along with the taxes that supported it, and leave the states with the option of funding such spending themselves. Ford pilloried the idea on the campaign trail and narrowly beat Reagan for the nomination that summer.

In the fall of 1977, when Kemp-Roth got its endorsement from the Republican National Committee, Reagan spoke up forcefully for it on the radio. "Twice in this century," he said on one of his weekly syndicated addresses, "in the 1920s and early 1960s"—a reference to Mellon and Kennedy—"we cut taxes and the stimulant to the economy was substantial and immediate. . . . Jack Kemp's bill would reduce the deficit, which causes inflation because the tax base would be broadened with the increased prosperity. We should help him."[2]

Reagan would seek the Republican nomination for president in

1980 not only because he had narrowly lost in 1976. By 1980, stagflation had devolved to such a depth, after the inflationary recovery of
1976–78, that it was clear that the incumbent president, Jimmy Carter,
was going to be driven from office in a rout.

In 1979 and 1980, the economy of the United States did something
it had never done, outside of wartime or war demobilization, since the
beginning of the official statistics back in 1913. It recorded two consec-
utive years of double-digit inflation. In 1979, consumer prices went up
by 11 percent. In 1980, they jumped by 14 percent. As for economic
growth, minus federal expenditures it was barely positive in 1979 and
sharply negative, by about 4 percent, in 1980. Two million workers lost
their jobs from June 1979 to June 1980. The National Bureau of Economic Research made it official: there was a recession in 1980, the year
of the highest peacetime inflation rate ever. The term "stagflation" no
longer captured the magnitude of the problem. The economy was not
stagnating, but shrinking in the context of unheard-of inflation.
Okun's misery index zoomed to an unthinkable 21.

Meanwhile, bracket creep plowed enormous amounts of inflation-
compensating income into the federal treasury. Federal receipts in
1980 were the most as a percentage of national economic output since
World War II, with the exception of one year (1969) at the peak of Vietnam. Yet the federal deficit cleared $70 billion in 1980, the fourth-
highest level in real terms since World War II.

In the presidential election year of 1980, the economic accounts of
the nation were in complete disarray, joblessness was hitting eight
million people, and the idea of getting ahead or even keeping in place
was made ludicrous by double-digit inflation and bracket creep. The
cause of the problem could not be hung on oil anymore. In 1980, a
barrel of petroleum was up an incredible elevenfold since 1973. But
gold more than matched that, as Roy Jastram knew it would. Gold
soared to over $800 per ounce in 1980, up more than twenty times
since 1971. Investors were pulling their funds out of enterprises and

into protective positions. Adjusted for inflation since the 1966 peak, the stock market indexes were down 70 percent by the spring of 1980.

The policy mix of the United States during the 1970s, the stagflation decade capped off by the lurid year of 1980, was loose money and high taxes plus government spending. The ending of gold redemption in 1971 gave the Federal Reserve autonomy to pursue any sort of monetary policy it wished. Through 1979 and the Fed chairmanships of Burns and Miller, the Fed had showed no inclination to follow any rule. It lowered interest rates and expanded the monetary base persistently, occasionally drawing back as the big inflation numbers came in, but loosening quickly as the unemployment and the negative growth followed. It had a preference in the 1970s for inflation over unemployment. It got both.

The progressive income tax ensured that the accommodation of inflation resulted in one of two outcomes regarding the federal treasury: Either federal revenues would boom, as bracket creep translated the cost-of-living increases of the American workforce into higher levels of taxation. Or federal revenues would sag, as earners preferred to take a lower standard of living than work extra-hard for raises that went mainly to the government. Both scenarios played out against each other through the stagflation decade, with the general trend being flat federal receipts, until the burst in 1980 caused by the 14 percent inflation. Both scenarios also implied poor real-world economic growth. If bracket creep did collect more revenue, it meant that the private sector was losing ground to the public; if it did not, it meant that a general economic strike was occurring.

In his 1978 memoir *A Time for Truth,* former Ford treasury secretary William E. Simon called what was going on "a structural war against the economy conducted by the state." The loose money discouraged investment in private, profit-seeking enterprises, because it was probable that the dollar would be worth less in the future. The inflation-fueled high marginal tax rates then further constricted the private sector. The unemployment that came forth prompted the government to spend on ameliorative programs, beyond even what the receipts procured by bracket creep could cover. This led to further governmental displacement of the private sector, of the real economy. It should have been clear by 1980 what had gone wrong. The United States had adopted the wrong policy mix.[3]

Yet certain prominent Democrats were cautioning that conditions were not right for a reapplication of the John F. Kennedy policy mix. Walter Heller hammered away in the *Wall Street Journal* (and contrary to his private advice to Ford in 1974), writing that the conditions of the early 1960s were totally different. There was "slack" in the economy twenty years prior, but not now—the evidence being the nosebleed inflation rate. Heller did not explain how the burst in unemployment that accompanied the inflation, the essence of stagflation, did not reflect slack. Democratic representative Thomas J. Downey of New York turned his back on the JFK tax cut in 1981, writing in the *New York Times* that "all the evidence shows that the Kennedy tax cut did *not* achieve growth without inflation." He pointed to the 1969 inflation rate—without observing that by that time, not only had the monetary half of the JFK policy mix been left a dead letter, but there had been a tax increase.[4]

Jimmy Carter named Paul Volcker as Federal Reserve chair in the summer of 1979, Carter's second appointment to that position. Carter asked Miller to step down from the Fed, where he had been all of sixteen months, to become treasury secretary, after Carter had fired Michael Blumenthal on account of another oil price increase from the Iranians. Volcker immediately and persistently tried to implement the monetary half of the old 1960s policy mix. He raised interest rates in 1979, acquiesced to Carter's request for limits on bank lending in 1980, and restricted the money supply in 1981. "Tight money" it was, but inflation stayed in the double digits. Volcker's first several years at the helm of the Fed showed that monetary vigilance, on its own, will not be effective unless accompanied by growth-oriented fiscal policy. Tax rate cuts spark private demand for the dollar by providing incentive for new economic activity. It is easy to adjust monetary policy given a marginal tax cut: supply the dollar as much as the market wants. The result will be noninflationary growth.

Carter was not going to cut tax rates, committed as he was to increasing tax progressivity—even though as his hopeless reelection prospects became clear in the summer of 1980, he floated the idea of some sort of general 5 percent cut in income taxes. Reagan was campaigning (though not at all times clearly) on Kemp-Roth. His main policy adviser, Martin Anderson, had outlined the priorities of the Reagan candidacy in a 1979 memo called "Policy Memorandum No. 1." The first item in the plan was to "reduce federal tax rates." The idea was fleshed out: "We must have a program—of at least three years' duration—of across-the-board tax cuts. The personal income tax rate must be cut by a specific percentage every year for three years, especially the higher, incentive-destroying marginal rates. . . . Tax rates that are too high destroy incentives to earn, cripple productivity, lead to deficit financing and inflation, and create unemployment." This was Kemp-Roth; but to any degree that Reagan incorporated members of the Nixon-Ford establishment into his campaign, pressure would mount to reconsider fiscal priorities along traditional Republican balanced-budget lines.[5]

As the campaign moved into 1980, it became clear with television commercials run in New Hampshire and Wisconsin from February through April that Reagan favored a large tax rate cut and a dollar strong against gold. These commercials explicitly compared Reagan's tax plans with those of John F. Kennedy. In both states, Reagan enjoyed distinct support from lower-income voters and Democrats who crossed over to vote Republican. Pollsters discovered that Reagan's commercials were more popular among Democrats than among Republicans. "Journalists were truly amazed at how lifetime urban Democrats were going bonkers for Reagan, and they began to specu-

late that Reagan was no Goldwater," as political historian Craig Shirley has written.[6]

During the Pennsylvania primary campaign in April 1980, Reagan's
opponent George H. W. Bush introduced a line that remains a slur
against supply-side tax cuts to this day. At a speech at Carnegie Mellon
University in Pennsylvania, Bush spoke of Reagan's "voodoo economic
policy." The tax rate cut would cause a budget deficit—this was the
traditional worry of old-fashioned Republicans—and the deficit would
in turn cause inflation. There would be too much extra spending in the
economy because of the tax cut and budget deficits. Bush's advisers
(culled from the Ford administration) calculated the effect. A 30 percent tax rate cut would cause the inflation rate to go up in an identical
manner. Reagan's tax cut would cause a 30 percent inflation. The accu-
sation did not sound entirely wild, because through the first quarter of
the year in 1980, inflation was running at an annual rate of 19 percent.

Bush won the Pennsylvania primary on April 22. Two days later, in
a debate in Bush's hometown of Houston, Reagan and Bush tangled
on the matter of tax cuts, supply-side economics, and the John F. Kennedy legacy. Bush jeered at Reagan that "you cite the Kennedy tax cut.
There wasn't any surplus then—there was a deficit resulting from that
scheme." He said that "it is my understanding that the Kennedy tax
cut resulted in a $4.4 billion deficit. . . . And it is my perception that
that tax cut applied today in the same percentages . . . would result in
an inflation rate of about 30 to 32 percent."[7]

Reagan countered with an explanation that his across-the-board,
10-10-10 rate cut would return to earners only part of the bracket-creep
gains that government was going to collect anyway over the next several years. He did not, however, pick up on the central flaw, the contraction, in Bush's argument. If the tax rate cut would cause a budget
deficit that in turn would cause a 32 percent inflation, bracket creep
would kick in to such a prodigious degree that the deficit would be
wiped out. An average 32 percent cost-of-living increase for American

earners in the early 1980s, unthinkable as that might be (but necessary
to sustain the 32 percent inflation that Bush foresaw), would have resulted in something approaching double the federal revenues—even
with a 10-10-10 tax rate cut in the progressive tax schedules.

As for Bush's claim that the Kennedy tax cut resulted in a $4.4 bil-
lion deficit (in the same debate he called it a $4.4 billion revenue loss),
it is not clear where he could have gotten those numbers. The official
government statistics on the matter published in January 1980 showed
that the federal deficit fell from $5.9 billion in 1964 (a fiscal year that
ended in June 1964) to $1.6 billion in 1965, as the tax cut was phased in.
The deficit the next year was $3.8 billion. As for federal revenues, they
grew in real terms at the gigantic rate of 8.8 percent per year from 1963
to 1967, moderating only with the LBJ income tax surcharge of 1968. In
Pennsylvania and Texas in April 1980, incidentally, Bush said that he
was "the supply-sider in this race," the one in favor of "supply-side tax
cuts"—the kind that go to businesses. Jude Wanniski regretted that he
had ever popularized the term.[8]

It is curious that the "voodoo" charge has lived on to this day as a
favorite epithet of opponents of supply-side economics and tax rate
cuts. In office in the 1980s, Reagan did cut tax rates, and major deficits
did come to pass. The mega-inflation of the previous generation, however, ceased to exist. Inflation collapsed by 75 percent in 1982–83, after
years of 7–14 percent increases, and has not been heard from since.
Bush's estimate of a 32 percent inflation, given Kemp-Roth, was off by
a factor of 10. Justifiable complaints have arisen that Haitian Vodou
religion does not deserve to be called on (indeed stigmatized) in the
wholly inapplicable field of American political-economic debate. This
point has special force, given the breathtaking inaccuracy of Bush's
original charge.

Reagan won the nomination over Bush that summer, picked Bush
as his running mate, and thereby brought Republicans into his circle
who were dubious about his tax rate cut. Alan Greenspan (who had

been Ford's CEA chair), Senator Robert Dole of Kansas (Ford's running mate in 1976), and others tried to dilute or forestall the cut from within the Reagan and Republican camps. Reagan easily won the election in November against Carter, and then had to put forth a plan.

On February 18, 1981, a month into his presidency, Reagan announced that he was seeking the 10-10-10 tax rate cut. The next day, he told reporters, "Back when Calvin Coolidge cut taxes across the board . . . the government's revenues increased. When Jack Kennedy did it . . . , his economic advisers, they were all telling him . . . that the government would lose $83 billion in revenue, and the government gained $54 billion in revenue. . . . So they had made quite a sizable financial error in their estimates. Jack Kennedy's line about it was, 'a rising tide lifts all boats.' And this is what we believe the tax proposals, that we've made, what they're aimed at."

Some supply-siders, in particular Kemp and Laffer, were hoping that Reagan might cut tax rates even more. They got an assist from an unlikely source. In March, Democratic representative William Brodhead introduced an amendment that effectively called for the three years' worth of cuts on the very top income tax rate, the rate of 70 percent, to come all at once. He wanted the maximum rate of the income tax taken down to 50 percent at the beginning of the new year, January 1, 1982.

It was unclear what Brodhead was up to. He represented a section of Detroit, a city that, thanks to stagflation and 22 percent interest rates—the prime rate of interest actually hit 22 percent in December 1980, meaning that mortgage rates, auto loans, and so on all began *above* that rate—was starting to collapse like it had in the recession of 1957–58. Brodhead said that the country needed more investment, rates from 50 to 70 percent only applied to dividends and capital gains, hence his proposal. Political columnists Rowland Evans and Robert Novak were not so sure. They thought that it was a Democratic ploy to prevent the across-the-board 10-10-10 rate cut. The Brodhead amendment, Evans and Novak suggested, could peel off Republican support for the general cut in income tax rates, on "supply-side" grounds that Bush had introduced the previous April—investment tax cuts were good for business. Reagan would be faced with the Brodhead amendment or no tax cut at all, he would have to sign it, and Kemp-Roth would be dead.

Kemp squelched that possibility by signing on as a cosponsor of the Brodhead amendment. He touted it as an essential complement to the 10-10-10 cuts for all rates below the 50 percent level. Then, on March 30, Reagan was shot and nearly killed in John Hinckley's assassination attempt. Without question, the outpouring of sympathy for the president in the aftermath of this event buoyed support for his tax-cut plan.

In the negotiations with Congress that spring and summer, the Brodhead amendment got folded into the final bill. Compromises included a delay in the effective date and the initial stage of the tax cut. There would be a 5 percent rate cut effective October 1, 1981, a 10 percent rate cut on July 1, 1982, and a 10 percent rate cut on July 1, 1983, with the adjusting of tax brackets for inflation (called "indexing") beginning in 1985. Congress passed the law with supermajority support. Nearly all Republicans and over half the Democrats voted for it. Reagan signed the Economic Recovery Tax Act (ERTA) at his Santa Barbara, California, ranch in August.

The similarities with the Revenue Act of 1964 were striking. Under ERTA, the average tax rate cut, across the board, was 23 percent. The arithmetic is 0.95 (a 5 percent cut) times 0.9 times 0.9 (two 10 percent cuts) equals 0.77, or a cut of 23 percent from the whole. This was essentially the average of the across-the-board rate cuts of 1964–65. As for the top rate, it went down from 70 percent to 50 percent on January 1, 1982. This was a cut in the top rate exactly equal, to four decimal places on a percentage basis (of 28.57 percent), to JFK's proposal of a cut in the top rate from 91 to 65 percent. After the full phase-in of

5-10-10 under ERTA in 1984, however, real tax rates on most earners would still be a little higher than they had been in 1965. Inflation had been that bad in the interim. Today the only provision of ERTA that is still law is the one that indexes the income tax code for inflation.

In September, Reagan addressed the criticism that Bush had aired the previous year that the tax cut was likely to exacerbate inflation. "There is . . . that question in people's minds," he said in remarks at an event in Chicago. " 'Can you cut taxes and fight inflation by so doing?' Well, I very much believe that you can. Let me just read you something. 'Our true choice is not between tax reduction on the one hand and the avoidance of large federal deficits on the other. An economy stifled by restrictive tax rates will never produce enough revenue to balance the budget, just as it will never produce enough jobs or enough profits.' John F. Kennedy said that back in 1962, when he was asking for a tax decrease, a cut in tax rates across the board. And he was proven right."[9]

The Reagan presidency entered its most difficult and harrowing months in the fall and winter of 1981–82. A recession the likes of which the United States had not seen since the 1930s came on the scene. In the six months beginning in October, the economy shrank at an annual rate of 5.6 percent. This was the worst six-month performance since the recession of 1957–58. There was no recovery to speak of in the remainder of 1982. By the end of the year, the nation's economy had not grown from the bottom reached nine months before. The economic dislocations across the country were easily the most severe since the Great Depression. By early 1983, unemployment in the seven counties surrounding the steelmaking region of Pittsburgh was 18 percent. Heavy industry had at last despaired of the economic conditions prevailing in the long era of stagflation and embarked upon layoffs of enormous magnitude. National unemployment peaked at 12 million in late 1982. This is a level, controlled for population growth, matched but not cleared at the trough of the Great Recession in 2009. The unemployment rate peaked at 10.8 percent in the recession of

1981–82, worse by almost a point than the highest level of 2008–9. Inflation in 1981 came in again at a double-digit rate, 10 percent, moderating to 6 percent the next year.

Why was the recession occurring—why did ERTA and "Reaganomics" (a new term in 1981) not forestall it? The first problem was that there was no real tax cut in 1981. The 5 percent cut effective in October 1981 was a 1.25 percent cut for the whole year—when inflation ran at 10 percent. There was not a tax cut, but another real tax increase in 1981, tacked onto the previous fifteen straight years of bracket creep. The second problem was the monetary half of the policy mix. Paul Volcker's Fed began tightening money again in the summer of 1981, just as in 1980. Real interest rates soared into the double digits as the money supply became static. Money was scarce and expensive, while tax rates were high—this de facto policy mix was in place in late 1981 and early 1982, during what still today may be spoken of as the worst recession since the Great Depression.

Certain Republicans (including Larry's boss at the OMB, David Stockman) turned their backs on the Reagan model. The recession was so deep by 1982 that lukewarm supporters of ERTA wanted the future installments of its income tax rate cuts canceled. The argument was that the budget deficit, plowing over $120 billion per year (again over half as big as Carter's most excessive) was spooking the financial markets and the economy to such a degree that investment had ground to a halt. The budget deficit was causing the recession. Reagan fought off appeals to nix or reduce the 10 percent cut in income tax rates scheduled for July 1, 1982, and for July 1, 1983, as well as the indexing of the tax brackets for inflation set for 1985. To do so, he had to compromise. He signed a bill permitting increases in excise taxes (and scrapping depreciation reform) in the summer of 1982, in lieu of modifying the income-tax-cut schedule of ERTA.

Meanwhile, Volcker had despaired of overtight money. The sky-high real interest rates were killing borrowers in the Third World, particularly Mexico. If the United States kept the clamps on the money supply, global insolvency could result. So Volcker started to loosen in the summer of 1982, increasing quantity targets and lowering interest rates. Arthur Laffer and Charles Kadlec wrote a series of pieces on Robert Bartley's page in the *Journal* proposing a theory regarding Volcker's moves. Whenever commodities, particularly gold, fell in price that summer, Volcker would supply more money. Whenever such things rose in price in the private markets, Volcker tightened. The Fed was applying an external rule as it conducted monetary policy—the first evidence of such a thing since the shutting of the gold window in 1971 and the onset of the stagflation era.

It was not only Mexican borrowers who had good use for the cash. Reagan's firmness on not canceling the big forthcoming rate cuts of ERTA, the major rate cuts scheduled for mid-1982 and mid-1983 and then inflation indexing beginning in 1985, meant that individuals were expecting better rates of return on investments, salary increases, and entrepreneurial ventures. People now had a chance to keep a decent share of new money they might earn, after the long stagflation interregnum—so they sought it out. The policy mix of the John F. Kennedy era was at last taking shape once again, a decade and a half after its first season in the sun. Tax rate cuts—a big 10 percent income tax rate reduction came on July 1, 1982—coupled with monetary policy tracking gold meant that the United States was, as of the summer of 1982, reprising the policy posture of both Kennedy's 1960s and Andrew Mellon's 1920s.

The stock market, which went up by 30 percent over the last five months of 1982, is one of the classic "leading indicators" of general economic trends. The late 1982 surge was just such a thing. Economic growth in 1983 and 1984 took off stratospherically. In the first quarter of 1983, real economic growth was 5.3 percent, followed by five con-

secutive quarters of growth over 7 percent—the only time that this
has ever happened in the history of the statistic. After the huge growth
of 1983–84, growth held at the robust level of 4 percent per year for the
remainder of the 1980s.

It was one of the greatest recoveries in American economic history.
Nineteen million new jobs emerged in the tremendous expansion, increasing the employment level of 1980 by a fifth. The expansion was
noninflationary. The double-digit inflation of 1979–81 vanished, giving
way to a 3 percent average increase in consumer prices from mid-1982
through the end of the decade. Economic growth was huge and inflation
lower than at any point since the immediate wake of the Kennedy tax
cut. Stagflation, that bitter chapter of American economic history, that
bane of the American dream, was (as Great Britain's Margaret Thatcher
said would be the fate of communism) sent off to the ash heap of history.

Prosperity came to the country as it had in the 1960s. Median family
income began a major leap up. Business formation exceeded the 1970s
level wildly. Savings grew abundantly in the bank (thanks to the stable
dollar) and there was a fourfold increase in the stock market (thanks to
the growth boom). African Americans benefited from the expansion just
as in the 1960s, as the black middle class emerged into substantial size.
The difference with the 1960s was that twenty years of the welfare state
had done its work enervating working-class and black culture. Had Kennedy been a little quicker with the tax cut in the early 1960s, perhaps he
would have staved off the push for welfare, LBJ's "bride," altogether.

The Democrats were sufficiently connected to their history in the
1980s to want to see the tax-cut job completed. Reagan's ERTA law in
1981 enjoyed the support of more than a hundred Democrats in Congress. A good number of these were southerners, "Boll Weevil Democrats," as they called themselves. With civil rights an accomplished
fact in law since 1965, holders of the congressional seats of former segregationists saw no reason not to prefer a booming economy. The
Democratic constituency most reluctant to embrace the John F. Kennedy economic policy had turned.

In 1985, the House Ways and Means Committee chairman (and Wilbur Mills's heir), Representative Dan Rostenkowski, Democrat of Illinois, teamed up with fellow party members Representative Richard Gephardt of Missouri and Senator Bill Bradley of New Jersey to introduce a bill that would reduce tax rates, especially the top rate, even more than had been done in ERTA, in exchange for loophole-closing. It was an attempt to complete what John F. Kennedy had initially aspired to. In April 1961, Kennedy introduced his tax-cut plan as a package containing the elimination of loopholes. His adviser on this matter, Stanley Surrey, coined the term "tax expenditures" to describe special carve-outs in the code that necessitated higher rates on everyone else. In the 1960s, Kennedy only got the rate cuts, not the loophole/tax expenditure closing. In the 1980s, a powerful cadre of congressional Democrats would get both.

Reagan was gleeful. In his 1986 State of the Union address, Reagan urged the American people to get behind the effort, and he cited Kennedy. As Reagan said before Congress that night, "The most powerful force we can enlist . . . is an ever-expanding American economy, unfettered and free. . . . I believe our tax rate cuts for the people have done more to spur a spirit of risk-taking and help America's economy break free than any program since John Kennedy's tax cut almost a quarter century ago."

Reagan continued: "Now history calls us to press on, to complete efforts for a historic tax reform." To Kemp's happy surprise (Kemp felt Reagan had not taken the top rate down far enough in 1981), negotiations in Congress yielded a final bill where the top rate was reduced all the way to 28 percent. In the most expansive visions of the supply-siders in the 1970s, it was never contemplated that a Democratic House (and a Republican Senate) would put such a bill on the president's desk by the mid-1980s. Yet it happened. The Tax Reform Act of 1986 had a top income tax rate of 28 percent and just one other rate, 15 percent. The income tax code was now set to be a combination of low and flat rates to a degree not seen since the first drawing of the income tax in 1913, when rates maxed out at 7 percent. Loopholes were closed, to the consternation of lobbyists. Inside operators in Washington had tried to stop the 1986 reform, as related in a bestselling book of the time called *Showdown at Gucci Gulch*. How were the lobbyists going to afford all their super-expensive Gucci threads if the top rate was so low that special interests would lose interest in seeking exemptions from it? The lobbyists might have to get a job in the real world—which, as it happened, was booming.

It must be stressed that the Tax Reform Act of 1986, whose signature feature was a reduction in the top rate to 28 percent, the fourth-lowest ever, represented the greatest example of bipartisan agreement and accomplishment in American economic policy arguably over the entirety of the twentieth century. The vote in the Senate in favor of the bill was 97–3, with liberal Democratic lions Edward M. Kennedy, Joe Biden, Paul Sarbanes, Chris Dodd, Al Gore Jr., and John Kerry all voting for.

As for the inspiration of the rate cut and reform, Bill Bradley, he remains the last politician until Vermont senator Bernie Sanders comfortable with being called a democratic socialist. Bradley had voted against the Reagan tax cut in 1981, because he wanted a tax plan that explicitly routed out loopholes for the rich while getting all rates down to a low flat level, the dream of Democrats since their founding in the nineteenth century and the party's standard preference since, notwithstanding the outrider Franklin D. Roosevelt. Bradley set to thinking how to do this after the Reagan tax cut passed. As the authors of *Showdown at Gucci Gulch* discovered, in his idle hours as a professional basketball player with the New York Knicks in the early 1970s, Bradley (a Princeton grad and a Rhodes Scholar) had "read Milton Friedman . . . and was fascinated to learn that a flat-tax system with a rate of just over 20 percent would raise as much money as the existing high-rate system. He also read about the largely fruitless efforts"—though Surrey certainly had gotten high rates cut—"of Stanley Surrey, the Harvard Law School academic who worked to reform the income tax in the 1960s."[10]

Bradley represented the explicit way that Democrats and Republicans could come together on tax policy. Low tax rates devalue exemptions, which makes them easier to kill (the 70 percent rate of the Kennedy tax cut was not low enough to really extinguish exemptions as Surrey desired), while pushing people to act on their economic initiative. And flat tax rates treat all citizens the same. Growth and fairness—that was the essence of low and flat tax rates. Bradley brought everyone into the tent in agreement.

The compromise that Kemp and the supply-siders had to countenance was a raising of the top capital gains tax rate from the ERTA level of 20 percent back up to the Steiger-amendment level of 28 percent. Reagan's vice president, George Bush, vowed that he would get that rate taken back down once he became president. This was presumably becoming a foregone conclusion, given the success of the Reagan economic policy after two terms.

There were big federal budget deficits in the Reagan era, about $175 billion per year. Commentators complained that "grandchildren" would be left with the bill. It didn't happen—economic growth was too great. By 2001, the Federal Reserve was worried that there was no longer enough U.S. government debt outstanding for the Fed to function in its buying and selling of the debt in the open market.[11]

Incredible transformations overtook the American economy. The old hedges against the dollar, the investment hideouts of the 1970s, lost their luster. Oil fell by more than half from the 1980 peak, just as did gold. Money shifted out of these inert assets and into stocks, bonds, and titles to enterprise, now that the dollar was strong and taxation would not confiscate the greater part of interest, dividends, and profits. The big surge in financial instruments in the 1980s, representing real businesses, secured retirements savaged by inflation. Entrepreneurialism flourished, as new enterprises from tech wizards Apple Computer, Sun Microsystems, Atari, and Fairchild spin-off Advanced Micro Devices to that humbler of the post office, Federal Express, elbowed their way into the Fortune 500. As prosperity came over the land again, as in the 1960s, the prospect had to be surer that the nation would try to keep it this time.

One of the most breathtaking developments in recent American political history is the unceremoniousness with which George H. W. Bush broke his promise—a promise as clear as they ever come in politics. Barely a year into his presidency, in the summer of 1990, Bush consented to an income tax increase, having said on his nomination for president in 1988, "Read my lips: no new taxes." As the old joke goes, you know a politician is fibbing when his lips are moving.

The tax increase Bush conceded to in 1990 was small, at the top only a three-point increase in the marginal rate. It was proffered by Democratic adversaries in Congress, ostensibly because of budget worries. The symbolic effect of this small rate hike was great, in that it effaced the signature of perhaps the greatest bipartisan tax bill of all time—the 28 percent marginal rate of the Tax Reform Act of 1986, which never had time to prove its worthiness. Lost in the shuffle was the fact that all the tax rate cuts of recent years—the JFK tax cuts, the capital gains cut of 1978, and the cuts of the 1980s—had proven themselves to be highly productive of revenue, not to mention economic growth. With George Bush, like with Nixon before, there was a reluctance to learn from the innovations of recent history. The halcyon Eisenhower days of his youth were to be his policy guide. A recession duly occurred in 1990–91, hitting right after the broken promise. The electorate hounded Bush from office the following year. He got 37 percent of the popular vote in his reelection bid, one of the worst totals of any incumbent seeking a second term.

This time, the JFK model would not wait a dozen some years to be reapplied, as in the 1970s. The interim would only be five years. Bush's successor, Democrat Bill Clinton, raised taxes again first thing in 1993, taking the top rate of the income tax to 39.6 percent. It was another repudiation of the Tax Reform Act of 1986. Economic growth over the tax-increase interregnum of 1990–93 was 2 percent per annum and inclusive of a recession—the old post–World War II standard that John F. Kennedy had shaken up.

The backsliding stopped in 1994, when Republicans took the whole Congress for the first time in forty years and made it clear to Clinton that he would neither increase spending nor do anything further on taxes outside of cut them. Federal spending decreased at the sharpest clip since the demobilization from World War II. In 1997, Congress presented the president with a capital gains cut, taking the top rate down again to 20 percent. Clinton signed it. In monetary policy, the Fed continued to conduct operations that were consistent with a low and stable price of gold and other major commodities. From 1994 to 2000, as the national debt was on a path to annihilation, the economy again grew at over 4 percent per year with inflation stable under 3 percent.

The tally from 1982 to 2000 reflected the patterns of the 1920s and 1960s. When the policy mix of the strong, stable dollar in concert with tax rate cuts (and their precursors in spending restraint) was in place, the long stretches of 1982–89 and 1994–2000, noninflationary growth above 4 percent per year prevailed. During the interregnum of questioning the low-tax-rate consensus, 1990–93, growth was weak, as in the 1970s and the 1950s.

This is the paramount lesson of the economic history of the United States since the nation chose, in 1913, to have the two institutions of macroeconomic policy, the Federal Reserve and the income tax. It is the model: when the Fed and the income tax are modest, the economy roars; when they are activist, the economy reels. JFK captured this model and made it his own in 1962. Reagan linked back to Kennedy in the 1960s, and Mellon in the 1920s, and did the same thing in the 1980s. The achievement was so impressive that the Republican Congress and President Clinton joined to keep it going in the 1990s.

The 2000s, our own era, have been one of the sorriest episodes in modern American economic history. Growth even before the 2008 col-

lapse barely cleared 2 percent per year. The recession of 2008 saw fifteen million go unemployed and untold numbers drop out of the
workforce. Since the beginning of the recovery in 2009, growth has
averaged 2.1 percent, and the workforce continues to fail to attract par-
ticipants. In the 1920s, the 1960s, and the 1980s, growth out of the
deepest low points of recession was epic, 6 or 7 percent, moderating to
4 percent for the duration. Not so the years after 2009. Growth was
poor out of the trough and stayed so.

The policy mix that John F. Kennedy rejected has saddled the American economy for this entire millennium. After President George W. Bush's
largely nonmarginal tax cut of 2001 (which took the top rate down all of
0.5 points to start with and bloated the code with credits and exemptions),
growth remained so sluggish that the Fed departed from its nineteen-
year tradition. It expanded money without regard to price increases in
gold and primary commodities. Tremendous capital reallocation into the
old inert dollar hedges came about. There were huge increases in the
prices of gold, oil, and land—the root of the housing bubble.

In 2008, as the crisis that became the Great Recession hit, the Fed
loosened money beyond all precedent. The only hint of John F.
Kennedy–style tax policy as the nation struggled with the immense
contraction of 2008–9 was President Obama's postponing for a year, in
2010, a scheduled 4.6-percentage-point increase in the top income tax
rate. In 2013, that and other tax rates went up, as the Fed held interest
rates at all-time lows and monetized debt like never before. Over
seven years of slow-growth recovery not even worthy of the name
from the Great Recession, the associated policy mix has been Fed activism and increases in tax rates. The secret of postwar prosperity, the
JFK-Reagan policy mix, has now gone dormant for the longest stretch
since it first came on the scene midway into the Kennedy presidency
in the summer of 1962.

THE TASK AHEAD

John F. Kennedy's presidency occurred before his party was transformed by the radicalism of the 1960s, before the Democrats became the party that both lost interest in economic growth and suspected that growth was exacerbating a problem—that of environmental degradation. From the 1970s to the 2000s, in a shift that would have puzzled if not revolted Kennedy, the Democrats increasingly became the party of growth scolds and as advocates of using the tax code to generate new preferences. Moreover, by the 2000s, they were content to have the Republicans identify with the tax-cut cause, perceiving that cuts in tax rates on the next dollar of income one stood to make could be interpreted as conferring a special benefit to go-getters and those who know how to help themselves, as opposed to the little guy.

With respect to the other half of the policy mix, a strong and stable dollar, Democrats in this millennium have preferred loose money from the Fed, with no suggestion of an external monetary standard, such as gold or commodities. Again, this is a break from the original tradition of the party. From the 1820s through the 1960s, the typical Democratic view was that lack of soundness in the currency will harm the working classes the most, because they are not schooled in the arts of playing financial hedges.

The generation of Kennedys on the public scene in the 2000s has been mystifyingly reliable in getting the great forebearer's policy wrong. In 2003, for example, the president's brother Senator Edward M. Kennedy and daughter, Caroline, wrote to an associate of Laffer's, Stephen Moore, "to request [that his group] withdraw any political advertising that uses President Kennedy's name and image to support [the] tax cuts" currently being debated, which were in fact tax rate cuts. The letter went on to recite the standard characterization of the

JFK tax cut, that its "tax benefits" went "primarily to lower and middle income working families" and that the national debt was negligible when Kennedy made his move. All incorrect, except in the sense that JFK's rate cuts on all earners, in particular on high earners, made the benefits—of economic growth—flow beautifully toward "working families."[1]

Beyond the Kennedy clan, the mainstream media, the *New York Times* in particular, has had its own trouble with the history of the JFK tax cut. When Paul Samuelson died in 2009, the *Times* obituary reported that he had "told the young president-elect that the nation was heading into a recession and that Kennedy should push through a tax cut to head it off. . . . Kennedy eventually accepted the professor's advice and signaled his willingness to cut taxes, but he was assassinated before he could take action"—no cognizance of JFK's introduction of the massive rate-cut bill (Samuelson having little if anything to do with it) in January 1963. "His successor, Lyndon B. Johnson," the *Times* staggered on, "carried out the plan, however, and the economy bounced back." The national paper of record had not clarified matters since 1987, when in its obituary for Heller it said that "the economic policies of the Kennedy . . . years were essentially built on the theory of John Maynard Keynes."[2]

The history of what happened half a century ago must be reclaimed as America continues to suffer through the intolerable sluggishness and diminishment of opportunity of the 2000s. JFK joined a bipartisan consensus as he ran for president in 1960, decrying economic mediocrity and calling for large, comprehensive, and sustained economic growth. In devising and applying his solution to this problem as president, Kennedy exposed the ridiculously high income tax rates at the top, rates up to 91 percent, for what they were.

These high rates were, first, a means of conferring value upon exemptions that sweetheart insiders in the corporate/Washington nexus could sneak into the statute book—an intolerable offense against equality. And they were, second, a means of diverting the cash flow and assets of the rich into profitable-enough (for them) evasion strategies as opposed to investment into real enterprises that created a broad prosperity. Appallingly, back in the 1950s and early 1960s, neither stodgy corporate bigwigs nor union bosses minded this state of affairs very much. Corporations, knowing that innovative new companies could eat their lunch, perceived that high rates stifled the accumulation of venture capital and lowered the real rate of profit of firms that could not get pet tax exemptions passed into law. Unions played along, doling out what jobs there were to the favored few in their membership, reserving ever-rising structural unemployment for African Americans and newcomers to the workforce.

The effect of the multidecade rate-cut era begun by JFK in 1962, interrupted as it was in the 1970s, was the simultaneous blooming of entrepreneurialism and an immense increase in jobs, most of them in much smaller businesses than the bureaucratic outfits that dominated the American scene in the 1950s. Sometimes Americans today get nostalgic for the job-for-life patterns of big corporate employment of yesteryear, as well as the protective cover of unions, which by the 1990s had essentially vanished from the private economy. JFK showed us, however, that those "good things" of the 1950s and early 1960s were creatures of the tax code and masked a deal with the devil. Big corporations and big labor conspired with a cautious government to get, via high tax rates, slow growth. Not only were untold start-ups never conceived or begun, but the civil rights revolution was kept at bay as a class of poverty-enmeshed citizens grew well into the tens of millions.

The two great noneconomic benefits of the two long tax-rate-cut periods, the 1960s, and the 1980s and 1990s, were the completion of the civil rights revolution and the restoration of the Soviet empire to freedom. The broad prosperity that followed the establishment of the JFK and then the Reagan economic policy mix cannot have been incidental to these developments, as both presidents envisioned. Prosperity has proven to be not merely an economic good in American life. It has proven to be an essential component of American identity, such that the nation expands the range of its human potential when economic growth runs its natural course.

How could we possibly not wish to follow this lead well into the 2000s, one of the worst eras of economic growth in all of American history, and as the populace of this nation has at turns in recent years become irascible and pessimistic, if not despondent? Think of the problems we could overwhelm:

1. Joblessness and underemployment, today affecting tens of millions. The JFK policy mix quadrupled the rate of job growth.
2. Budget deficits and debt. The deficits of the 1980s were so outdistanced by economic growth that by 2001 the prospect arose of a market bereft of government debt.
3. Inequality. If ever there was an unequal income tax system, it was that of the 20–91 percent "paper rates," where the high earners hid their money on the swindle sheet, and the diversion of capital to unproductive resources gave us "the other America" of structurally unemployed and poor. JFK's rate cuts put the rich's capital to work in the real economy, and it delivered the most beloved prosperity to the middle class of all time.
4. Entitlements. Social Security and Medicare would not only become solvent with economic growth, but ever more unnecessary as the American people become prosperous and able to innovate better solutions for old age than bureaucratic government programs.
5. Health care. The king of all loopholes is the health insurance deduction that keeps tax rates excessively high. This is now joined by the "tax cliffs" of the Affordable Care Act that make the poor face the highest real tax rates in the code. Cutting tax

rates and sweeping out regulations would incur organic reform in the health care market.

6. Student loans. LBJ was so clueless that he thought the youth would stay unemployed given the JFK tax cut and ramped up the draft. Today we have student loans to keep young people away from a workforce that outnumbers jobs available. The policy mix, applied again today, would attract students into the workforce and force colleges to compete by meeting students at their ability to pay.

7. Environment. The heart of economic growth is innovation, doing far more with the same or even less. Real environmental progress is inseparable from economic growth.

What of the cavils of economists who say that good growth rates are not possible anymore, that it is irresponsible to call for 5 or 6 percent growth, that "secular stagnation" is the "new normal"? Economics whiffed on getting policy right in the JFK years, and we were lucky we had a president then who could choose the one right plan from among all the confusion. In the 1970s, economics was even more embarrassed as the Keynesian playbook was reopened and stagflation resulted. The profession has never made peace with the phenomenal success of the Reagan revolution. It should be held to account until it corrects its models.

The historical narrative we two authors have written here, we believe, is a teaching moment of acute interest and necessity in the second decade of a new millennium in which economic growth has been a rarity, the recessions nasty, and the ranks of the struggling and disaffected getting ominously more numerous. The JFK-Reagan model has, alas, been abandoned over the last two decades. Tax rate cuts, a sound dollar, government spending that goes down on account of economic growth, free trade (it was Kennedy who spurred the biggest round of tariff reductions of modern times), a reliance on the market as opposed to regulation to discover best practices—above all the deep desire to see this country grow, and in growing be itself—this is the model to which we must return in order to shift into prosperity once again.

Prosperity used to be thought of as the nation's lot, as its birthright. At JFK's inaugural, the poet Robert Frost spoke of "the gift outright," meaning the land, this continent, given to us Americans so that we might to do great things with it and on it. Kennedy was crestfallen, when he ran for and won the presidency, that the nation was not doing much with that gift, instead getting by with a mediocre economy. Then he did something about the problem. His initial choices included their share of mistakes, but his own sense of clarity drove him toward the inevitable conclusion: usher the government out of the way, for America to be America. There can be no question what John F. Kennedy would say to us today, were he here in anticipation of his hundredth birthday: it surely is time, once again, "to get this country moving again."

Acknowledgments

Larry writes: First, I'd like to thank Art Laffer, who is really the god-father of this project and who has been such a dear friend and mentor over these many years. There are many other free-market supply-siders, too numerous to name, who have pointed us in the right direction. Thank you all. Much appreciation to Susan Varga, my longtime friend and indefatigable business manager. And to Wayne Kabak, my friend and agent, who helped change my life and career in wonderful ways I never dreamed possible. And I must thank my coauthor, Brian Domitrovic, for his superb historiography, which became the glue holding this book together. Most important, I thank my saintly wife, Judith Pond Kudlow, who is the core of my heart and soul. I love her, and always will.

Larry and Brian would like to thank Stephanie Ferrell, our research assistant while she was an undergraduate at Harvard, who examined the archives at the JFK Presidential Library with expertise and efficiency.

Brian writes: I appreciate the support of my institutions, Sam Houston State University, the University of Colorado, and the Laffer Center at the Pacific Research Institute. Another big thank-you is owed to Art Laffer, who, along with Robert A. Mundell and the late Robert L. Bartley, has made a priority of caring not only for supply-side economics per se but for its history. I would like to make special mention of Katherine Pierce, Robert M. Collins, and Joshua Melnick for their helpful comments, as well as my agent, Michael Carlisle. Books are largely put together at home, and the four ladies at my house helped see this work through; thanks, my dears! At Larry's place, Judy did the same thing as we authors logged the good hours together, discovering and fashioning this history.

Appendix: Marginal and Corporate Tax Rates Before and After the Revenue Act of 1964

Before the Revenue Act of 1964

Federal Individual Income Tax Rates

RATE	INCOME BRACKET
20%	$0 to $2,000
22%	$2,000 to $4,000
26%	$4,000 to $6,000
30%	$6,000 to $8,000
34%	$8,000 to $10,000
38%	$10,000 to $12,000
43%	$12,000 to $14,000
47%	$14,000 to $16,000
50%	$16,000 to $18,000
53%	$18,000 to $20,000
56%	$20,000 to $22,000
59%	$22,000 to $26,000
62%	$26,000 to $32,000
65%	$32,000 to $38,000
69%	$38,000 to $44,000
72%	$44,000 to $50,000
75%	$50,000 to $63,000
78%	$60,000 to $70,000
81%	$70,000 to $80,000
84%	$80,000 to $90,000
87%	$90,000 to $100,000
89%	$100,000 to $150,000
90%	$150,000 to $200,000
91%	Over $200,000

Top Corporate Tax Rate
52%

Top Capital Gains Tax Rate
25%

After the Revenue Act of 1964

Federal Individual Income Tax Rates

RATE	INCOME BRACKET
14%	$0 to $500
15%	$500 to $1,000
16%	$1,000 to $1,500
17%	$1,500 to $2,000
19%	$2,000 to $4,000
22%	$4,000 to $6,000
25%	$6,000 to $8,000
28%	$8,000 to $10,000
32%	$10,000 to $12,000
36%	$12,000 to $14,000
39%	$14,000 to $16,000
42%	$16,000 to $18,000
45%	$18,000 to $20,000
48%	$20,000 to $22,000
50%	$22,000 to $26,000
53%	$26,000 to $32,000
55%	$32,000 to $38,000
58%	$38,000 to $44,000
60%	$44,000 to $50,000
62%	$50,000 to $60,000
64%	$60,000 to $70,000
66%	$70,000 to $80,000
68%	$80,000 to $90,000
69%	$90,000 to $100,000
70%	Over $100,000

Top Corporate Tax Rate
48%

Top Capital Gains Tax Rate
25%

After the Economic Recovery Tax Act of 1981

Federal Individual Income Tax Rates

RATE	INCOME BRACKET
0%	$0 to $2,300
11%	$2,300 to $3,400
13%	$3,400 to $4,400
15%	$4,400 to $8,500
17%	$8,500 to $10,800
19%	$10,800 to $12,900
21%	$12,900 to $15,000
24%	$15,000 to $18,200
28%	$18,200 to $23,500
32%	$23,500 to $28,800
36%	$28,800 to $34,100
40%	$34,100 to $41,500
45%	$41,500 to $55,300
50%	Over $55,300

Top Corporate Tax Rate
46%

Top Capital Gains Tax Rate
20%

After the Tax Reform Act of 1986

Federal Individual Income Tax Rates

RATE	INCOME BRACKET
15%	$0 to $17,850
28%	Over $17,850

Top Corporate Tax Rate
34%

Top Capital Gains Tax Rate
28%

Note: Individual tax rates are based on single or married filing separately.

Notes

Primary-source statistics come from the standard econometric datasets, including those at the websites of the Bureau of Labor Statistics, the Bureau of Economic Analysis, the Census Bureau, www .measuringworth.com, the Federal Reserve Bank of St. Louis (FRED database), *Historical Statistics of the United States* (Millennial Edition, 2006), and each year's *Budget of the United States Government*. Voting histories are from https://www. govtrack.us and *Congressional Quarterly*. Presidential oratory and presidential messages to Congress are drawn from the Public Papers of the Presidents at the American Presidency Project (APP) website, http://www.presidency.ucsb.edu. When the date is given in the text, the speech may be found by that date on the APP website. Otherwise the speech is referenced with a note. The campaign speeches of 1960 are also housed on the APP site and may be found by a search controlling for the date. Presidential libraries referred to in the notes are the John F. Kennedy Presidential Library, Boston; the Lyndon B. Johnson Presidential Library, Austin, Texas; and the Gerald R. Ford Presidential Library, Ann Arbor, Michigan. Important secondary literature in addition to those works referenced in the notes includes Robert M. Collins, *More: The Politics of Economic Growth in Postwar America* (New York: Oxford University Press, 2000); Herbert Stein, *The Fiscal Revolution of America: Policy in Pursuit of Reality* (Washington, DC: AEI Press, 1996); and Ira Stoll, *JFK, Conservative* (New York: Houghton Mifflin Harcourt, 2013).

Introduction

1. Tom Wolfe, *Hooking Up* (New York: Farrar, Straus & Giroux, 2000), 3.

Chapter 1: Stormy Weather

1. "Kennedy Promises Jobless Plan Shortly," *Wall Street Journal,* January 20, 1961; Bernard D. Nossiter, "Concern Voiced by Kennedy on Slump, Jobless," *Washington Post,* January 20, 1961.
2. Theodore C. Sorensen, *Kennedy* (New York: Harper & Row, 1965), 240.
3. "The Key," *Wall Street Journal,* January 2, 1953. See also Chris Roush, *Thinking Things Over: Vermont Royster's Legacy at the Wall Street Journal* (Portland, OR: Marion Street Press, 2014).
4. President's Press Conference, February 17, 1953, APP.
5. *Chicago Defender,* February 22, 1958.
6. Warner Bloomberg Jr. and Victor F. Hoffmann Jr., "The Recession Hits Gary, Indiana," *Commentary* 26, no. 1 (July 1958): 16–17.
7. Michael Harrington, "Our Fifty Million Poor: The Forgotten Men of the Affluent Society," *Commentary* 28, no. 1 (January 1959): 19; Dan Cordtz, "Auto Capital Battles Slump Problems with Public, Private Help," *Wall Street Journal,* March 24, 1958.

Chapter 2: Path to Power

1. Margaret L. Coit Oral History Interview—JFK #1, 6/1/1966, section 4, John F. Kennedy Presidential Library.
2. Philip W. Magness, "From Tariffs to the Income Tax: Trade Protection and Revenue in the United States Tax System" (PhD dissertation, George Mason University, 2009), 149.
3. David Nasaw, *The Patriarch: The Remarkable Life and Turbulent Times of Joseph P. Kennedy* (New York: Penguin Press, 2012), 195–96.
4. Ibid., 132, 213.
5. Robert Dallek, *An Unfinished Life: John F. Kennedy, 1917–1963* (New York: Little, Brown, 2003), 64.
6. David Pitts, *Jack and Lem: John F. Kennedy and Lem Billings: The Untold Story of an Extraordinary Friendship* (New York: Carroll & Graf, 2007), 80.
7. Rockefeller Brothers Fund, *The Challenge to America: Its Economic and Social Aspects* (Garden City, NY: Doubleday, 1958), 22–23.
8. "The Platform Statements by Rockefeller and Nixon," *New York Times,* July 24, 1960.
9. "Question and Answer Session . . . Seattle WA," September 6, 1960, APP.
10. Sorensen, *Kennedy,* 217; G. Scott Thomas, *A New World to Be Won: John Kennedy, Richard Nixon, and the Tumultuous Year of 1960* (Santa Barbara,

CA: Praeger, 2011), 257; Richard M. Nixon, *Six Crises* (Garden City, NY: Doubleday, 1962), 310.

11. "Presidential Debate in Chicago," September 26, 1960, APP.

Chapter 3: Advisers

1. James Piereson, *Camelot and the Cultural Revolution: How the Assassination of John F. Kennedy Shattered American Liberalism* (New York: Encounter Books, 2013), 188, 194.

2. Robert D. Novak, "Kennedy's Braintrust: More Professors Enlist but They Play Limited Policy-Making Role," *Wall Street Journal*, August 4, 1960.

3. Richard Austin Smith, "The Fifty-Million-Dollar Man," *Fortune*, November 1957, 177.

4. Irving Bernstein, *Promises Kept: John F. Kennedy's New Frontier* (New York: Oxford University Press, 1991), 127.

5. C. Douglas Dillon Oral History Interview—JFK #1, 7/30/1964, John F. Kennedy Presidential Library.

6. James Tobin, "Growth Through Taxation," *New Republic*, July 25, 1960, 17–18.

7. *Two Revolutions in Economic Policy: The First Economic Reports of Kennedy and Reagan*, ed. James Tobin and Murray Weidenbaum (Cambridge, MA: MIT Press, 1988), 4.

8. "Kennedy Asks Backer of Low-Money Rate, Budget Surplus to Head Economic Council," *Wall Street Journal*, December 20, 1960.

9. William L. Cary, "Pressure Groups and the Revenue Code: A Requiem in Honor of the Departing Uniformity of the Tax Laws," *Harvard Law Review* 68, no. 5 (March 1955): 745.

10. Stanley S. Surrey, "The Federal Income Tax Base for Individuals," *Tax Revision Compendium* (Washington, DC: Government Printing Office, 1959), 2, 13–14.

11. Taxation Task Force, "Tax Policy for 1961," Task Force Reports, Transition Files, Taxation Task Force Reports, John. F. Kennedy Presidential Library, 94, 97.

12. Paul A. Samuelson, "Prospects and Policies for the 1961 American Economy: A Report to President-Elect Kennedy," Transition Files, Task Force Reports, Economy—Samuelson Report, January 1961, John F. Kennedy Presidential Library, 2, 3, 7, 10; reprinted without underscores in "Text of Report to the President-Elect on Prospects for Nation's Economy in 1961," *New York Times*, January 6, 1961.

13. Edward A. Behr, "Treasury Triangle," *Wall Street Journal,* December 19, 1960.

14. Richard Reeves, *President Kennedy: Profile of Power* (New York: Touchstone, 1994), 18.

15. Arthur M. Schlesinger Jr., *A Thousand Days: John F. Kennedy in the White House* (Boston: Houghton Mifflin, 1965), 643.

Chapter 4: A Keynesian First Year

1. "Kennedy Asks Faster Economic Growth, but Offers No Specific Goal or Method," *Wall Street Journal,* September 6, 1960.

2. "Senate Unit Barrages Nominee for Tax Post with Hostile Questions," ibid., March 23, 1961.

3. Surrey et al. quoted in Joseph J. Thorndike, *Their Fair Share: Taxing the Rich in the Age of FDR* (Washington, DC: Urban Institute Press, 2013), 258.

4. Theodore H. White, *The Making of the President 1964* (New York: Atheneum, 1965), 26.

5. Walter W. Heller, "CED's Stabilizing Budget Policy After Ten Years," *American Economic Review* 47, no. 5 (September 1957): 645.

6. *Economic Report of the President, 1962* (Washington, DC: Government Printing Office, 1962), 108.

7. Christina Romer, "A Look Inside the Economic Report of the President," https://www.whitehouse.gov/blog/2010/02/11/a-look-inside-economic -report-president; *Economic Report of the President, 1962,* 130.

8. See C. Douglas Dillon Personal Papers, Boxes 33 and 34, John F. Kennedy Presidential Library.

9. "Business Views May Settle Fate of Tax Program," *Wall Street Journal,* May 15, 1961.

10. "Dillon Predicts U.S. Economic Boom By Mid-'62," ibid., June 21, 1961.

Chapter 5: A Turning Point

1. Details of the steel crisis are in Bernstein, *Promises Kept,* chapter 4.

2. Allen J. Matusow, *The Unraveling of America: A History of Liberalism in the 1960s* (Athens: University of Georgia Press, 2009), 37.

3. Benjamin C. Bradlee, *Conversations with Kennedy* (New York: W. W. Norton, 1975), 76–77.

4. Wallace Carroll, "Steel: A 72-Hour Drama with an All-Star Cast," *New York Times,* April 23, 1962.

5. "Special Message to the Congress on Taxation," April 20, 1961, APP.

6. Paul A. Samuelson, "Memorandum for the President and Council of Economic Advisors," Box 20, F "Recovery Program 3/31/61," 1, Walter W. Heller Personal Papers, John F. Kennedy Presidential Library.

7. Dillon's cover letters and markups of the BIS and IMF reports: Papers of John F. Kennedy, Presidential Papers, President's Office Files, Departments and Agencies, Treasury, June 1962, John F. Kennedy Presidential Library.

8. Robert A. Mundell, "On the History of the Mundell-Fleming Model," *IMF Staff Papers* 47 (Special Issue, 2001): 221–22.

9. *New York Times,* June 15, 1962.

10. Quoted in "White House Outgoing Message," Heller-JFK, June 29, 1962, Box 22, F "Tax Cut, 6/62–7/62," Heller Papers, John F. Kennedy Presidential Library.

11. "The President's News Conference," July 5, 1962, APP.

Chapter 6: JFK the Tax-Cutter Finds Himself

1. "White House Outgoing Message," 3.

2. Memo, Dillon-JFK, June 6, 1962, Box 34, F "Tax Cut, 6/62–7/62," Dillon Papers, John F. Kennedy Presidential Library; memo, Dillon-JFK, July 12, 1962, F "July 1962 (1)," Treasury Memoranda to the President, Dillon Papers, ibid.

3. *The Presidential Recordings: John F. Kennedy: The Great Crises,* vol. 1, *July 30–August 1962,* ed. Timothy Naftali (New York: W. W. Norton, 2001), 337, 339, 380–81.

4. Reeves, *President Kennedy,* 334; Heller, "Memorandum for the President: Stand-by Tax Authority," August 16, 1962, Box 21, F "Stand-by Tax Authority, 1/62–6/64," Heller Papers, John F. Kennedy Presidential Library; memo, Heller-Kennedy, August 10, 1962, Box 22, F "Tax Cut, 8/62," ibid.

5. "Statement by the President upon Signing the Revenue Act," October 16, 1962, APP.

6. Theodore C. Sorensen, "Notes for Tax Cut Speech," 7, Box 67, F "Economic Report to Congress/Memoranda and Speech Materials, 12/11/62–1/17/63," JFK Speech Files 1961–63, Theodore C. Sorensen Papers, John F. Kennedy Presidential Library.

7. "Question and Answer Period: Economic Club of New York," Box 42, F "Economic Club of New York, 12/14/62: Speech Materials and Press Release," JFK Speech Files 1961–63, John F. Kennedy Presidential Library.

Chapter 7: The Push Begins

1. *Economic Report of the President, 1963*, xvii.
2. "Statement of Hon. C. Douglas Dillon, Secretary of the Treasury," *President's 1963 Tax Message* (Washington, DC: Government Printing Office, 1963), Part 1, 29.
3. Geoffrey J. Lanning, "Some Realities of Tax Reform," *Tax Revision Compendium*, 20.
4. "Custodian of Quality," *Wall Street Journal*, January 16, 1963.
5. "The Other Side of the Ledger," ibid., January 15, 1963.
6. *President's 1963 Tax Message*, Part 1, 534.
7. "Dillon to Discuss Tax Bill with House Unit at Closed-Door Sessions Starting Tuesday," *Wall Street Journal*, March 28, 1963.
8. "Administration May Continue Accelerated Public Works Spending," ibid., February 11, 1963.
9. Robert D. Novak, "House Unit Is Divided by Issue of Gradual or One-Shot Rate Slash," ibid., April 22, 1963.
10. "Forecasts of 1963 National Product Being Boosted," ibid., April 22, 1963.

Chapter 8: The Civil Rights Connection

1. Robert D. Novak, "The Negro Vote," *Wall Street Journal*, October 25, 1960.
2. William P. Jones, *The March on Washington: Jobs, Freedom, and the Forgotten History of Civil Rights* (New York: W. W. Norton, 2013), Kindle ed., Loc. 2315.
3. Ibid., Loc. 2629.
4. Michael Harrington, *The Other America: Poverty in the United States* (New York: Penguin, 1986), 31, 33, 146, 153.
5. "Byrd Warns Civil Rights Debate May Snag Tax Bill," *Wall Street Journal*, June 11, 1963; "Kennedy Given Notice: Byrd on Anniversary Reaffirms Tax Stand," *Washington Post*, June 11, 1963.
6. C. P. Trussell, "Jobless Are Denied Aid as House Vote Rebuffs Kennedy," *New York Times*, June 13, 1963.
7. Jones, *The March on Washington*, Loc. 2471–82.
8. Tom Wicker, "Kennedy Renews Plea for Tax Cut to Bar Recession," *New York Times*, June 9, 1963.
9. "House Committee Tax Provisions Explained," *Congressional Quarterly Weekly Report* 37, no. 34 (August 23, 1963): 1474.
10. Jones, *The March on Washington*, Loc. 3042–63.
11. Richard Reeves, *President Kennedy: Profile of Power* (New York: Touchstone, 1994), 585.

12. Jones, *The March on Washington*, Loc. 3392–402.
13. "Tax Cut, Reform," *Congressional Quarterly Weekly Report* 37, no. 37 (September 13, 1963): 1562.
14. The intertwined legislative history of the tax cut and civil rights is discussed in Ted Gittinger and Allen Fisher, "LBJ Champions the Civil Rights Act of 1964," *Prologue* magazine 36, no. 2 (Summer 2004).
15. "House Rejects Recommittal; Votes Tax Cut, 271–155," *CQ Almanac 1963*, 19th ed. (Washington, DC: Congressional Quarterly, 1964), 486–99, http://library.cqpress.com/cqalmanac/cqal63-1315751.
16. "Rockefeller Criticizes President's Actions on Balance of Payments; Offers Own Plan," *Wall Street Journal*, September 3, 1963; "Rockefeller's Budget for Fiscal '64 Is Facing Cuts by GOP Rebels," ibid., March 22, 1963.
17. *Congressional Quarterly Weekly Report* 37, no. 39 (September 27, 1963): 1695.
18. "Interview on NBC's 'Huntley-Brinkley Report,'" September 9, 1963, White House Audio Recordings, 1961–1963, John F. Kennedy Presidential Library.
19. Gore to JFK, November 15, 1962, Treasury Memoranda for the President, Box 34, F "Nov. 1962–January 1963 and 1962 undated," Dillon Papers, John F. Kennedy Presidential Library.
20. "Dillon Sees No Reason at This Time to Fear Inflationary Price Push," *Wall Street Journal*, October 18, 1963.
21. "Democrat Recants His Tax Cut Tactics," *New York Times*, October 22, 1963.
22. Thurston Clarke, *JFK's Last Hundred Days: The Transformation of a Man and the Emergence of a Great President* (New York: Penguin, 2014), 311.

Chapter 9: Bill's Passage

1. Barry Goldwater, *Senator Goldwater Speaks Out on the Issues* (Washington, DC: Goldwater for President Committee, 1964), 19.
2. "Handle with Care," *Wall Street Journal*, February 27, 1964; "The Kennedy-Johnson Tax Bill," *New York Times*, February 26, 1964.
3. *Economic Report of the President, 1964*, 7–8.
4. Tom Wolfe, *Hooking Up* (New York: Farrar, Straus & Giroux, 2000), 19.

Chapter 10: Regression

1. "Lyndon Johnson and Richard Daley in the Oval Office on 17 August 1964," Conversation WH6408-25-4978, 4979, 4980, *Presidential Recordings of Lyndon B. Johnson, Digital Edition*, ed. David G. Coleman et al. (Charlottesville: University of Virginia Press, 2010).

2. "Telephone Conversation with Lyndon B. Johnson," November 25 and December 16, 1964, William McChesney Martin Collection, fraser.stlouisfed.org; Robert A. Caro, *The Years of Lyndon Johnson*, vol. 4, *The Passage of Power* (New York: Alfred A. Knopf, 2012), 423.

3. Louis L. Goldstein to Lyndon B. Johnson, January 15, 1964, LE/FI 11 1/9/64–2/14/64, Lyndon B. Johnson Presidential Library.

4. Council of Economic Advisers Oral History Interview—JFK #1, 8/1/1964, John F. Kennedy Library, 172, 440; *Look*, June 18, 1963.

5. Arthur M. Okun, *The Political Economy of Prosperity* (New York: W. W. Norton, 1970), 45.

6. Thomas McArdle, "Bobby Kennedy Savaged Big Government Like Today's GOP Never Would," *Investor's Business Daily*, October 19, 2015.

Chapter 11: A New Camelot

1. Thurston Clarke, *JFK's Last Hundred Days: The Transformation of a Man and the Emergence of a Great President* (New York: Penguin, 2014), 180.

2. Paul A. Samuelson, "Sustaining American Prosperity," November 17, 1964, Box 56, F "Final Report to the President of the Task Force on Sustaining Prosperity," 19, Dillon Papers, John F. Kennedy Presidential Library.

3. *Inside the Nixon Administration: The Secret Diary of Arthur Burns, 1969–1974*, ed. Robert H. Ferrell (Lawrence: University Press of Kansas, 2010), 59.

4. Robert A. Mundell, "The Dollar and the Policy Mix: 1971," *Essays in International Finance* 85 (May 1971).

5. Alan Reynolds, "The Case Against Wage and Price Control," *National Review*, September 24, 1971, 1051.

6. Robert A. Mundell, "Inflation from an International Viewpoint," in *The Phenomenon of Worldwide Inflation*, ed. David I. Meiselman and Arthur B. Laffer (Washington, DC: American Enterprise Institute, 1975), 144.

7. Jude Wanniski, "It's Time to Cut Taxes," *Wall Street Journal*, December 11, 1974.

8. Arthur Burns Papers, Box B24, File CEA 1974, Gerald R. Ford Presidential Library.

9. Details of Kemp's biography are drawn from Morton Kondracke and Fred Barnes, *Jack Kemp: The Bleeding Heart Conservative Who Changed America* (New York: Sentinel, 2015).

10. Personal collection of Morton Kondracke.

11. Jude Wanniski, "Taxes and the Kennedy Gamble," *Wall Street Journal*, September 23, 1976.

12. Robert L. Bartley, *The Seven Fat Years: And How to Do It Again* (New York: Free Press, 1992), 59.

13. "Tax the Rich!," *Wall Street Journal*, March 8, 1977.

14. Kondracke and Barnes, *Jack Kemp*, 45.

15. Ibid., 46–47.

16. Jimmy Carter, "Acceptance Speech: Our Nation's Past and Future," Democratic National Convention, July 15, 1976, http://www.jimmycarterlibrary .gov/documents/speeches/acceptance_speech.pdf.

17. Bruce Bartlett, *Reaganomics: Supply-Side Economics in Action* (Westport, CT: Arlington House, 1981), 121, 131; letter, Michael Blumenthal to Rep. John Rousselot, Feb. 28, 1977, Box 29, F "Budget Testimony Letters," John Rousselot Papers, University of Southern California, Los Angeles.

18. "JFK Strikes Again," *Wall Street Journal*, February 23, 1977.

19. "The 1979 Tax Increase," ibid., October 17, 1978.

Chapter 12: The Reagan Revolution

1. Rowland Evans and Robert Novak, *The Reagan Revolution: An Inside Look at the Transformation of the U.S. Government* (New York: E. P. Dutton, 1981), 32.

2. *Reagan, in His Own Hand: The Writings of Ronald Reagan That Reveal His Revolutionary Vision for America*, ed. Kiron Skinner, Annelise Anderson, and Martin Anderson (New York: Free Press, 2001), 277.

3. William E. Simon, *A Time for Truth* (New York: Berkley, 1979), 106.

4. Thomas J. Downey, "Inflationary Lesson of the Kennedy Tax Cut," letter to the editor, *New York Times*, May 12, 1981.

5. Martin Anderson, *Revolution: The Reagan Legacy* (Stanford, CA: Hoover Institution Press, 1988), 117.

6. Craig Shirley, *Rendezvous with Destiny: Ronald Reagan and the Campaign That Changed America* (Wilmington, DE: ISI Books, 2011), 235–36.

7. "Bush-Reagan Debate 1980 on Taxes," YouTube, https://www.youtube .com/watch?v=edchtf9MS7g.

8. *The Budget of the United States Government: Fiscal Year 1981* (Washington, DC: Government Printing Office, 1980), 614; Evans and Novak, *The Reagan Revolution*, 109.

9. "Remarks at the Illinois Forum Reception in Chicago," September 2, 1981, APP.

10. Jeffrey H. Birnbaum and Alan S. Murray, *Showdown at Gucci Gulch: Lawmakers, Lobbyists, and the Unlikely Triumph of Tax Reform* (New York: Vintage, 1988), 26.

11. Federal Reserve chairman Alan Greenspan in his April 27, 2001, speech

"The Paydown of Federal Debt" considered the possibility of a crimp in the Fed's operations because of the shrinking size of the public debt outstanding: http://www.federalreserve.gov/boardDocs/speeches/2001/20010427/default.htm.

Epilogue: The Task Ahead

1. Stephen Moore, "A Letter and a Legacy Denied," Laffer Associates: Supply-Side Investment Research, May 15, 2003.
2. Leonard Silk, "Heller Legacy: Clarity for All," *New York Times*, June 19, 1987; Michael M. Weinstein, "Paul A. Samuelson, Economist, Dies at 94," ibid., December 13, 2009.

Index